TAP INTO THE POWER SOURCE!

The Holy Spirit was sent to lead and guide believers in every area of their lives, i.e. their finances, marriages, careers, businesses, etc. When Christians give the Holy Spirit complete control of their lives and allow Him to do what He was sent to do they will be able to avoid the pitfalls of the enemy. When you are led by the Spirit you can mistake-proof your life!

Many believers are not experiencing the power and privilege of being led by the Holy Spirit on a daily basis. He is the underutilized power source in the lives of believers. Jesus told his disciples before and after His resurrection that He was going back to his Father and would send back the Holy Spirit. He knew believers could not live a victorious Christian life without the help of the Holy Spirit. Jesus sent believers the ultimate power source!

About the Author

Joyce has been commissioned by God to teach, exhort, and remind believers about the role the Holy Spirit should have in every believer's life and the powerful results they will experience when they utilize the Holy Spirit's power! She is a minister, teacher, author, life coach, conference speaker, and marriage counselor. In addition to her evangelistic ministry, she is the Executive Director of Joyce Lester Ministries and teaches a weekly Bible study on discipleship, healing and deliverance, and hosted a weekly television program.

ASK THE HOLY SPIRIT!

The POWER Source JESUS Provided

ASK THE HOLY SPIRIT!

The POWER Source JESUS Provided

Joyce Lester

Copyright © 2015 Joyce Lester.

A production of
J.L. Ministries

Located at
Joyce Lester Ministries
245 N. Ruth Street St. Paul, MN 55119
Tel: 612-250-8714
E-mail: joycelester@usfamily.net
Website: joycelester.org

All rights reserved. No part of this book may be used or reproduced by any means, graphic, electronic, or mechanical, including photocopying, recording, taping or by any information storage retrieval system without the written permission of the publisher except in the case of brief quotations embodied in critical articles and reviews.

WestBow Press books may be ordered through booksellers or by contacting:

WestBow Press
A Division of Thomas Nelson & Zondervan
1663 Liberty Drive
Bloomington, IN 47403
www.westbowpress.com
1 (866) 928-1240

Because of the dynamic nature of the Internet, any web addresses or links contained in this book may have changed since publication and may no longer be valid. The views expressed in this work are solely those of the author and do not necessarily reflect the views of the publisher, and the publisher hereby disclaims any responsibility for them.

Any people depicted in stock imagery provided by Thinkstock are models, and such images are being used for illustrative purposes only.
Certain stock imagery © Thinkstock.

ISBN: 978-1-4908-8005-1 (sc)
ISBN: 978-1-5127-0758-8 (e)

Library of Congress Control Number: 2015907287

Print information available on the last page.

WestBow Press rev. date: 02/23/2018

Scripture quotations are taken from the *Holy Bible, New Living Translation*, copyright © 1996. Used by permission of Tyndale House Publishers, Inc., Wheaton, IL 60189 USA. All rights reserved.

Editor: Gloria Larson

CONTENTS

1. Are You Utilizing The Holy Spirit's Power? — 1
2. The POWER Source JESUS Provided — 7
3. Why Jesus Sent the Holy Spirit — 14
4. The Role of the Holy Spirit — 22
5. Holy Spirit What Should I Do? — 29
6. Consulting Holy Spirit About Finances — 36
7. A Spirit Led Marriage — 42
8. Spirit Led Parenting — 52
9. Spiritual Guidance in Living Single — 61
10. Spirit Led Leaders — 71
11. Listening for Holy Spirit to Speak — 86
12. Patience to Wait — 93
13. Hindering the Power Source — 98
14. Desires — 106
15. The Power Flowing Through Me — 114

AUTHOR'S NOTE

One day after thirty-nine years of salvation, and seeing myself, as well as, many other believers living far beneath the promises and power Jesus provided, I asked God the question, "How is it believers have the power that raised Jesus from the dead living inside of them, yet they live such defeated lives?" He answered, "Because my people are trying to live a spiritual life without depending on my Holy Spirit."

After receiving my answer from God, He commissioned me to write this book to emphasize the role, importance and power of being led by the Holy Spirit. God said the reason His church is not impacting the world in the way it should is because believers are not operating in the supernatural power of God, and that can only happen when His children depend on, are controlled by, and obey the Holy Spirit.

When believers utilize the wisdom, power and guidance of the Holy Spirit our lives will be transformed and we live the new life that Jesus provided for us. Jesus sent the Holy Spirit so we can have victory in every area of our lives, and build His Kingdom on earth, but this is not possible unless we depend on His help. It is my prayer that after reading this book you will incorporate the Holy Spirit's leading in every decision you make. The Holy Spirit will work through you in ways you could never have imagined and He will help you fulfill your God-given destiny!

INTRODUCTION

Imagine a life where you don't have to struggle with problems any more. You can wake up each day with peace and joy regardless of the circumstances life presents you. You can live a life where you have a source that has the answers to all of your problems and will lead and guide you around and through the multiple obstacles of life. This source is all knowing and all powerful and when you follow the leading of this source you literally mistake proof your life. As a result you can avoid the painful consequences of wrong or poor choices. You are able to make the right decisions every time in the areas of finances, relationships, marriage, children, career, education, health, and more because this powerful source is guiding you.

What I have just described is not an imaginary life for those who chose to be led by the Holy Spirit, the gift Jesus Christ provided after His resurrection. It is possible and available to those who have accepted Christ as their Savior to have His Holy Spirit living on the inside of them. Many believers are either unaware or have never experienced this life because they have not heard of the role of the Holy Spirit or suppress the reality of the Holy Spirit's promptings. We are privileged to have this dynamite power operating in our lives on a daily basis.

I am not saying living a life being led by the Holy Spirit is a problem free life. John 16:33 Jesus said, "…here on earth you will have many trials and sorrows. But take heart, because I have overcome the world."

Jesus provided the power source that will allow believers the ability to prevent or overcome any obstacle life presents. In this book I will take you on a journey to show you the importance and powerful results of a life that is led by the Holy Spirit!

Chapter 1

Are You Utilizing The Holy Spirit's Power?

> Seek his will in all you do, and he will show you which path to take.
> *(Proverbs 3:6)*

Do you acknowledge God every time you make a decision? Do you ask God how to spend your money, what career you should have, what school you should attend, what person you should marry or be in a relationship with, how to raise your children, or what church you should attend?

Many Christians have married the wrong person, bought the wrong house, purchased the wrong car, accepted the wrong job, and the list goes on. Then they spend a lot of time crying to God about the problems because of their self-centered decisions. Some people spend years in struggles and heartache because of wrong choices. It also causes many believers to be defocused from God's kingdom building work. This of course is the enemy's ultimate goal because He knows <u>when believers are walking in power and victory in their lives they will be able to influence others and teach them how they too can walk in victory.</u>

I was talking to a sister in Christ about being led by the Spirit and she said, "I was taught by my mother and grandmother that we are to step out and do something first then God will help us." It reminded me of a saying I heard in a church that promoted the same thinking, "If you make one step God will make two." In other words, act before consulting God and then when it doesn't work out people expect God to fix it. This ideology is self-driven.

Throughout Scripture there are many references to following God's leading and instruction to us to always ask the Lord to lead us through the Holy Spirit. In some instances we don't even have to ask Him if we truly let Him lead, because <u>Holy Spirit speaks to us about all situations, we just have to be sensitive to listen.</u> Unfortunately, we are often distracted by our desires or other's opinions that we miss what He is telling us to do.

Distractions come in many forms and believers are turning to the ways of this earthly world. Believers fall into the trap of being led by horoscopes, psychics, superstitions, instincts, taking risks, peer pressure, new age meditation practices, relatives, friends, coworkers, the media, talk show hosts, church doctrine, family tradition, and a myriad of other sources.

ASK THE HOLY SPIRIT!

Jesus provided us with the perfect source for wisdom and direction regarding the will of the Father and His purpose and plan for every individual's life. All we have to do is ask the Holy Spirit to tell us God's will. Nevertheless, Christians are making many choices that are causing them unnecessary suffering from the consequences of those decisions. Whenever we ask, listen and obey the Holy Spirit's leading we can be assured that we will make the right choices every time. God's will is always in our best interest.

Whenever born again believers consistently ask the Holy Spirit, the power source that Jesus provided, what God's will is for each situation or concern they can literally mistake proof their life! For some, surrender and obedience comes easily and quickly and for others maturity takes years. Regardless of how long it takes, the path to living a holy life is God's will for every believer.

God has provided the way so we don't have to go through life making mistake after mistake. God told us to acknowledge Him and seek His will because He desires to show us the path we should take.

It is certain that any path God chooses will lead us to peace and victory. When our path becomes unfamiliar and uncomfortable we need to be guided by the Holy Spirit in order to ensure that each step is God ordered. He will provide step by step instructions in the process of growing our faith and dependence on him when we take the time to pray and ask the Holy Spirit to reveal God's will before we act.

Make it a habit to ask God daily to direct your life. Even though I have an appointment book and make plans I will change my plans if the Holy Spirit leads me to do something different. Does this mean we should not have a schedule? No, it doesn't mean we should not make plans, but we should always acknowledge God as we plan our lives. Believers often consult God only when things do not turn out the way they expected or when there is a crisis. If we depend on God, at all times, the plans we make through the Holy Spirit will be fulfilling and accomplish the work God has planned for us.

Holy Spirit is the power source that believers need to know more about and take advantage of the gifts He brings to every believer's life. If I had known in the beginning of my walk with God, after salvation, that I had access to this power source and truly understood what that meant, as I do now, my life would have looked very different.

I wouldn't have wasted so many years living beneath the privileges Jesus gave His life for in order to freely give them to us. But all is not lost and it is never too late to turn your life over to the leading of the Holy Spirit.

The Holy Spirit wants to be our power source, but He will not force Himself on us. If you want to receive the benefits of His presence you must become sensitive to Him. Begin by asking for His guidance, seeking His leading, and following His direction. At first, you may be unsure of what you hear but take a minute and pray, being sensitive to His leading brings peace and confidence, and trusting Him is not a feeling; it is all about faith.

My question to every believer is, "Are you asking the Holy Spirit to lead in order to tap into His power?" If not, start today and experience the wonderful results of this power source operating in your life.

> Whenever born again believers consistently utilize the POWER SOURCE that Jesus provided, they literally MISTAKE-PROOF their life!

Chapter 2

The POWER Source JESUS Provided

I have asked many believers if they are led by the Holy Spirit. Most say no, and sadly others admit they didn't even know they should be led by Him. Many believers are not experiencing the power and privilege of being led by the Holy Spirit on a daily basis.

Jesus told His disciples before and after His resurrection that He was going to send a Helper, the Holy Spirit. Jesus said the Counselor would lead and guide us into ALL truth.

The power source Jesus provided, is the third person of the Trinity; the Holy Spirit. He is a person equal in every way with the Father and the Son. All of the divine characteristics associated with the Father and the Son are relevant to the Holy Spirit.

The Holy Spirit came to glorify Christ and to lead believers into all truth. The Holy Spirit came to give us the power to live and share the abundant life Jesus promised to all who trust and obey Him. We cannot live the abundant life without the help of the Holy Spirit.

What does it mean to be led by the Holy Spirit? Being led by the Spirit simply means to consult the Holy Spirit in all we say and do, then listen for His direction and obey His leading. It also means that He must be in control of our lives all the time.

Counseling believers over the past twenty years has revealed to me that the Holy Spirit, God's power source, is underutilized by so many believers. Imagine if all believers availed themselves to all the Holy Spirit is able to do; evil in this world would lose its powerful hold on people. Unfortunately, many believers have not been taught or are not aware that it is possible to have His power active in and through them all the time.

If an individual is afforded an unlimited source that would make their life much simpler, easier, carefree, and powerful, but chooses not to take advantage of that source, they would be considered foolish. Observers would be puzzled and question why that person continues to struggle with unnecessary pain, heartache, confusion, disappointment and lack, when all they have to do is to tap into their unlimited power source – Holy Spirit.

God is concerned about everything that concerns us. Many believers limit their experience with the Holy Spirit to what happens in their local church. Too often they don't include God in their daily activities. He is our heavenly Father and He doesn't want us faltering and failing in life. We spend a lot of time trying to figure out what to do when all we have to do is ask someone who has all the answers, the Holy Spirit.

The Holy Spirit was sent to help us navigate the twists, turns, and obstacles we experience in life. Jesus warned us that life is going to be filled with challenges, but with the spiritual weapons of prayer, fasting, and God's armor as described in Ephesians 6: 10-17 and the Holy Spirit we have been given all the tools, power, and authority to overcome any obstacle. However, to overcome obstacles we have to use the resources He has provided for us.

Before I came to the understanding of God's power, I often failed to consult the Holy Spirit about my problems and I have observed this in the lives of so many believers, as well. However, as I matured, I began to understand that the life of a believer should look totally different from the life of an unbeliever. The way we handle problems should be done according to God's instruction in the Word, as revealed to us by the Holy Spirit. The Holy Spirit will always direct us according to the scriptures and bring them to our remembrance. By allowing the Holy Spirit total access to direct our actions the full power to live a life pleasing to God is unleashed.

Jesus' death gave us direct access to the throne of God when Jesus breathed His last breath. The scriptures tell us God tore the curtain from the top to the bottom giving us full access and fellowship with the Father. We no longer need an earthly source to intercede for us because Jesus is sitting on the right hand of God advocating for believers.

Jesus also promised to send us a Helper, and His name is Holy Spirit, to dwell "in us" and "with us." The Holy Spirit gives us direct access to the Holy of Holies, which is the presence of God. That means we can have an audience with God whenever and wherever we need to. God is omnipresent; He is present everywhere at the same time. God is present in believers all over the world through His Spirit.

Before Jesus began His earthly ministry He too was baptized with water and the Holy Spirit. While in His fleshly body Jesus needed the POWER SOURCE operating in His life in order to fulfill His purpose for coming to earth. Jesus knew He would not have been able to do all the miracles, signs and wonders that He did without being led and empowered by the Holy Spirit. Jesus knew that it is the Spirit that gives us the power to operate in the spiritual realm and defeat evil principalities and powers.

Holy Spirit gives us power over the flesh and the demonic evil forces controlled by Satan. Sin no longer has control over us because Jesus destroyed the power of sin on the cross. We can walk in victory every day if we take advantage of what our Savior provided.

> When you follow the desires of your sinful nature, the results are very clear: sexual immorality, impurity, lustful pleasures, idolatry, sorcery, hostility, quarreling, jealousy, outbursts of anger, selfish ambition, dissension, division, envy, drunkenness, wild parties, and other sins like these. Let me tell you again, as I have before, that anyone living that sort of life will not inherit the kingdom of God.
> (Galatians 5:19-21)

Jesus also knew that as long as we are in our physical body we will be in a constant war against our fleshly desires. He knew in order for believers to take advantage of what He died for we were going to need a power greater than ourselves. That is why Jesus sent the Holy Spirit to indwell every believer. Many believers remind me of the children of Israel when God invited them to come to the mountain to talk directly to Him as recorded in Exodus 20:19 when they told Moses, "…you speak to us, and we will listen. But don't let God speak directly to us, or we will die." This type of fear is not from God. Sin and the lies of Satan in the ears of believers enforce worldly living versus a growing relationship with God. When things go bad it is easier to blame leadership than be accountable themselves, as did the children of Israel.

Even with this example many people and believers, even today, would rather have a pastor, bishop, apostle, evangelist, intercessor, or prophet, talk to God for them. What they don't understand is the same Holy Spirit that speaks through spiritual leaders will speak directly to them. I often remind Christians that just because a person has a title in front of their name does not necessarily mean they are being led by the Holy Spirit.

Therefore, if they are looking for someone else to keep them connected to God and if the person they are depending on becomes distracted by sin or is not walking in the Spirit, it will impact their life as well. When we know God for ourselves, He will never lead us away from His purpose for our lives.

I am grateful and count it a privilege and honor that God has commissioned me to spread this wonderful news about this great power source – the Holy Spirit, and encourage believers to tap into Him on a daily basis. What an assignment!

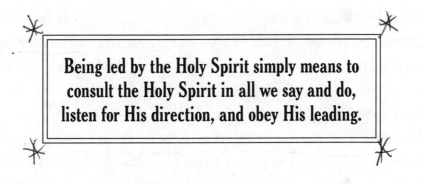

Being led by the Holy Spirit simply means to consult the Holy Spirit in all we say and do, listen for His direction, and obey His leading.

Chapter 3

Why Jesus Sent the Holy Spirit

In Acts 1:8, Jesus told the apostles, "But you will receive power when the Holy Spirit comes upon you..." Jesus gave us the Holy Spirit primarily so we could be witnesses about what Jesus has done to reconnect mankind back to God and to build His kingdom on earth, as it is in heaven. Every believer is supposed to be an ambassador for Christ. Jesus knew we would need power to do God's will, just as He did while He was here on earth. When Jesus was baptized in water the Holy Spirit rested upon Him and immediately led Him to fast for forty days and nights. Because Jesus followed the Holy Spirit's leading, He was able to touch the lives of countless individuals in His short time on earth.

Jesus is our perfect example of how we are to be in the world, but not of the world. Jesus expects us to follow his example. Jesus sent the Holy Spirit to empower us to live a holy life so we would be the light of the world, and the salt of the earth. Jesus knew we would not be able to do as He did without the power of the Holy Spirit.

Before I understood how to live a victorious Christian life through the guidance and power of the Holy Spirit, living life as a believer was not something I enjoyed. I was often focused on complaining about what Satan was doing to me. I wasn't excited about this new life that Jesus had provided for me. I spent years, as a miserable Christian.

I didn't grow up going to church; therefore, I didn't know what to expect. So, as a young believer I determined that Christian people should always be nice and happy. Well it didn't take me long to figure out I was wrong. The people in the church seemed to be just as unhappy as the people in the world. Most of the ones I encountered didn't seem excited about being a believer at all. They talked a lot about what the Devil was doing to them. They kept saying how happy they would be when they got to heaven. Eventually, I started acting just like them. I was indwelled by the Holy Spirit, but like others around me, I wasn't manifesting the fruit.

I needed to have my worldly thinking replaced and begin viewing the world from God's perspective. I needed someone to tell me that the power that raised Jesus from the dead is living inside me. I needed to know that no weapon that is formed against me by the enemy is going to prosper.

I needed to know that greater is He that is in me, than Satan, who is ruling the atmosphere of this world. Unfortunately, most of the believers I was around didn't know any more than I did. They were religious churchgoers that didn't know who they were in Christ or the power of the Holy Spirit.

Jesus Christ gave His life for us to be partakers of victory over sin and it can only be experienced by believers through obedience to the Holy Spirit. This would allow us to avoid a lot of heartache, struggle, pain, and unnecessary suffering. Christ has provided power, wisdom, and peace when problems arise, when we ask the question, "Holy Spirit what should I do?" When we walk in the Spirit and are led by Him and obey His leading we experience victory, after victory, after victory!

From the time we are born we are influenced by man's opinions. Then very early in life, as early as toddlers, we begin to develop opinions, likes and dislikes. We are born selfish and self-seeking. Scripture tells us that the flesh and God's Spirit are always in conflict. In order to trust the Lord with all our hearts, we cannot trust in our own wisdom, or the wisdom of this world. That is not to say that we cannot learn some good things from the world, but God's wisdom supersedes the world's wisdom. His wisdom is the filter that lets us know what we are to accept or reject from the world, teachers, and our spiritual leaders.

✳ True Wisdom Comes from God ✳

If you are wise and understand God's ways, prove it by living an honorable life, doing good works with the humility that comes from wisdom. But if you are bitterly jealous and there is selfish ambition in your heart, don't cover up the truth with boasting and lying. For jealousy and selfishness is not God's kind of wisdom. Such things are earthly, unspiritual, and demonic. For wherever there is jealousy and selfish ambition, there you will find disorder and evil of every kind. But the wisdom from above is first of all pure. It is also peace loving, gentle at all times, and willing to yield to others. It is full of mercy and good deeds. It shows no favoritism and is always sincere. And those who are peacemakers will plant seeds of peace and reap a harvest of righteousness.

(James 3: 13-18)

Consider it an awesome privilege and honor to be an ambassador for Christ. We can be effective representatives with the help of the Holy Spirit. When an individual is sent as an ambassador of a country, they are given specific instructions about their mission and they are expected to operate within those guidelines. It is the same with God's ambassadors. We are expected to follow his specific instructions when we are representing Him.

Jesus knew believers would not be equipped to stand for Him without the help and power of the Holy Spirit. Jesus told us to live according to the leading of the Holy Spirit because He knows that without Him our flesh will get in the way of us being vessels that He can use to build God's kingdom. When we accept Christ as our Savior and Lord, our hearts and minds have to be transformed and this can only take place if by faith we submit to being led by the Spirit.

When an individual is not saved he becomes skilled at walking in his own reasoning. Our lives are greatly influenced from what we have learned from the world. Therefore, after a person accepts Christ as their Savior they have to learn how to walk in the Holy Spirit and become knowledgeable about God's ways. To transition from the influence of the world, it is important for believers to remember that our thoughts need to be filtered through the Word of God. The Bible says believers have the mind of Christ, which means we have access to God's way of thinking. Whenever we make a decision our thinking should always be aligned with how God thinks.

However, some believers are seeking wisdom from this world through secular books, television talk shows, magazines, etc. Others are turning to advice offered by different religions and using the knowledge they gain from these sources to guide them. This is truly unfortunate considering the fact that believers have access to the highest wisdom available to man, which is the intelligence of God.

> Don't copy the behavior and customs of this world, but let God transform you into a new person by changing the way you think. Then

ASK THE HOLY SPIRIT!

> you will learn to know God's will for you,
> which is good and pleasing and perfect.
> (Romans 12:2)

When we accept Christ as our Savior we should no longer live according to the lifestyle of the world. We must continually renew our mind until we experience a spiritual metamorphosis; a complete change from the inside out. The key to this change is the "mind" the control center of one's attitudes, thoughts, feelings and actions. As our mind is made new by reading God's Word, praying, fasting, and being led by the Spirit, our lifestyle is being transformed. We will live a life that pleases God.

If we don't continuously ask the Holy Spirit to lead us we will be making crucial decisions based on our limited experience, our emotions, or the advice of others. Often, believers think or say they are suffering for the cause of Christ but actually they are suffering because of poor decisions or disobedience as a result of not consulting the Holy Spirit or not listening for His leading.

When I decided I no longer wanted to do things my way I prayed for God to shine a light in me and show me all of the areas in my life that were hindering my Christian walk. I had no idea when I prayed that prayer how much growing, cleansing, and pruning had to be done. It was a long and painful process because I was rebellious and wanted to do things my way. The tears I shed and being uncomfortable while learning a new way of life was worth it compared to living life without the relationship I now have with God. Not only did my relationship grow with God I grew in my love and relationships with the people God put in my life.

I have been transformed into a yielded and usable vessel for God. My desire is to live according to God's purpose, plan, and will for my life. During the time I was going through my transformation the Holy Spirit taught me many things regarding the will of the Father. I finally had enough reaping of painful consequences by making my own decisions. My only regret is that it took so long for me to gain this knowledge and finally realizing that I had it all along through the Holy Spirit. I am so grateful that God is a merciful and longsuffering God, and that He loves unconditionally.

> Jesus sent the Holy Spirit to empower us to live a holy life so we would be the light of the world, and the salt of the earth.

Chapter 4

The Role of the Holy Spirit

The role of the Holy Spirit is to lead, guide, teach and empower imperfect people in an imperfect world. Jesus sent the Holy Spirit to lead us into all truth.

The Holy Spirit is not a power or force, He is a person. Jesus continually referred to the Holy Spirit as "He", not "It".

> And I will ask the Father, and he will give you another Advocate, who will never leave you. He is the Holy Spirit, who leads into all truth….
>
> (John 14: 16-17a)

> But when the Father sends the Advocate as my representative—that is, the Holy Spirit—he will teach you everything and will remind you of everything I told you.
>
> (John 14:26)

ASK THE HOLY SPIRIT!

One day, the Holy Spirit told me it was not necessary for me to struggle to live a Christian life. He said I was trying so hard in my own strength, never including Him as my Helper, which caused me to be vulnerable to the enemy. I remember being on a spiritual roller coaster, as far as my emotions, when I responded to problems in life and I often felt frustrated or defeated. I had not grasped the concept of the Holy Spirit playing a daily role in my life.

Jesus said He would send us the Counselor who would lead and guide us into ALL truth. God has a master plan for every person's life and He wants to reveal it to us. We should always be listening for God's voice, as He speaks through the Holy Spirit.

God wants us to get our instructions from Him and obey what He tells us to do. Once I understood this, my Christian walk was no longer hard or difficult. Whenever I began to pray for God's direction and obey Holy Spirit's leading my life became filled with peace because He tells me exactly what, when, and how to handle every situation or circumstance. When I follow Him things turn out right every time. Scripture, God's Word, instructs believers to live by the Holy Spirit's power, not their own.

> So I say, let the Holy Spirit guide your lives. Then you won't be doing what your sinful nature craves. The sinful nature wants to do evil, which is just the opposite of what the Spirit wants. And the Spirit gives us desires that are the opposite of

what the sinful nature desires. These two forces are constantly fighting each other, so you are not free to carry out your good intentions.

(Galatians 5:16-17)

When we allow the Holy Spirit to lead us He gives us power over our desire to live as we want and as influenced by life around us. Self-centered living always craves disobedience toward the life God wants from us. This sinful nature is directly opposed to God's Spirit. As long as we are in these physical bodies there will be a war between our wants and desires and the Holy Spirit. Life requires us to make many choices every day, and those decisions should always be filtered through the Word and the Holy Spirit. The only spirit that is greater than the evil principalities, powers and wickedness we encounter every day is the Holy Spirit.

One day God gave me a revelation regarding the manifestation of the fruit of the Spirit in my life. I heard a message that encouraged the listeners to conduct a fruit inspection in their life and see how many they had and how many were missing. I proceeded to do a fruit inspection. Every time I would do my check list I would come up short or I would lose a check mark on a fruit that I was manifesting before because I would respond to a life circumstance in my own way. It was truly a frustrating cycle. I have heard many schools of thought regarding how spiritual fruit should be manifested in our life. But, the Lord told me that the way to allow the manifestation of the fruit of the Holy Spirit is to be controlled by the Holy Spirit.

ASK THE HOLY SPIRIT!

The Holy Spirit is the only one that can produce the fruit that is needed for whatever problem or situation we face. This understanding was so freeing for me, because now I understood how the process worked. I could not produce the fruit, which I had tried to do for so many years. This lifted a heavy burden from me because I was always struggling to get it right. Now, I know that the Holy Spirit has to produce the fruit, in me!

The functions and responsibilities of the Holy Spirit are important in the lives of believers. If we allow the Holy Spirit to control us we will avoid the pitfalls that Satan has planned for us. With the Holy Spirit's help we are able to walk in power and victory moment by moment. When we are led by the Spirit there will be times when the Holy Spirit will tell us to go in one direction but our personal knowledge and experiences can cause us to feel and do the opposite.

The Holy Spirit will always lead us to go against what feels right emotionally and intellectually and what the world says is right, because the Holy Spirit always directs us toward the Lord's perfect will for us. God has a master plan and the way to be sure we are operating according to His desires is to depend on the Holy Spirit. We have all made decisions that seemed right at the time but later discover they were wrong.

Some people think we are supposed to make a decision based on what we feel as the best choice. If things don't work out we go to God and ask for forgiveness, then ask Him what we should have done or what we should do to fix the problem. We don't have to keep making mistake after mistake. We can get it right the first time when we ask the Holy Spirit for God's wisdom.

> "My thoughts are nothing like your thoughts," says the Lord. "And my ways are far beyond anything you could imagine. For just as the heavens are higher than the earth, so my ways are higher than your ways and my thoughts higher than your thoughts."
> (Isaiah 55:8-9)

The Holy Spirit always leads us according to God's thoughts. He will never compromise Scripture. Jesus said on numerous occasions He did not come to do His will but His Father's will. This must be the attitude of a believer who wants to walk in the fullness of the Holy Spirit.

I have often thought to myself, if I had a dollar for every time I failed to consult with the Holy Spirit and made choices based on feelings, emotions, or circumstances, and suffered the consequences of doing so, I would be a wealthy individual. I also realize how much valuable time I have wasted reaping the consequences of wrong decisions.

One day after experiencing hurt, pain, and confusion, I finally decided, I was going to surrender to God's way.

I realized doing things my way, and repeatedly making mistakes was costly. I came to the conclusion that living life according to my terms was not worth the agony I had to endure, and I also realized the suffering was completely unnecessary. I wanted the abundant life that Jesus promised.

Over the years, I have heard many sermons and read in God's Word about the promises that were made to all believers. Through studying the Word and because of personal experiences, I now understand that every promise Jesus made has a stipulation. The word "if" usually precedes the promise informing us of what is necessary to receive the promise. Therefore, I began to ask Holy Spirit to give me direction because He knows all the "ifs" and will give us wisdom and power to carry them out. He knows that understanding the "if" is the key to receiving everything Jesus provided through the shedding of His blood. The enemy's goal is to distract us so we don't avail ourselves of these great and precious promises.

> The role of the Holy Spirit is to lead, guide, teach, and empower imperfect people in an imperfect world.

Chapter 5

Holy Spirit What Should I Do?

> Trust in the Lord with all your heart; do not depend on your own understanding. Seek his will in all you do, and he will show you which path to take.
>
> (Proverbs 3:5-6)

Jesus sent us the Holy Spirit to be our Counselor. It just makes sense to turn to the Holy Spirit whenever we need to make a decision or need direction. It takes less than ten seconds to ask the question "Holy Spirit what should I do?" If we ask this question in every situation we will stop making choices according to our will and emotions, resulting in repeated costly mistakes, and instead receive what's best for us every time.

And the Holy Spirit helps us in our weakness. For example, we don't know what God wants us to pray for. But the Holy Spirit prays for us with groaning that cannot be expressed with words. And the Father who knows all hearts knows what the Spirit is saying, for the Spirit pleads for us believers in harmony with God's own will. And we know that God causes everything to work together for the good of those who love God and are called according to his purpose for them."

(Romans 8:26-28)

Holy Spirit Leading Us in Giving

Believers that I have talked to think God wants us to just respond whenever we see a person in need and if we make a mistake He will fix it because our intentions were good or right. A believer asked my opinion about extending love and kindness to an individual who responded in an ungrateful and negative way. Most believers have experienced this at some point in their life while helping someone in distress. I told this individual that too often we make decisions based on our emotions then we get hurt by people we decided to help. I shared that there are two things God taught me about situations like this. One, in all things we are to ask God to direct our paths and this includes when we want to help someone who is in need. Secondly, when we consult the Holy Spirit, He will give us wisdom about who we should or should not help. This is a new concept for many believers and it changes lives.

As believers, we know that Satan comes as an angel of light and believers are often deceived because they are not discerning situations through the Holy Spirit. We can be doing a good deed and be out of God's will. I have personally experienced being hurt

by individuals whom I helped or made sacrifices to help them at a difficult time in their lives.

Most of the time I didn't consult the Holy Spirit and eventually I had experienced enough hurt to finally understood the importance of asking Him what I should do. When we do a kind deed because we are led by the Spirit we are doing so out of obedience to God, therefore it doesn't matter how the person responds because we are doing it "as unto the Lord."

Holy Spirit Leading Our Prayers

There are times when situations come up that seem so overwhelming we don't know what direction to take. We never have to avoid prayer because we don't know what to pray. The Bible tells us that the Holy Spirit will help us when we don't know what to pray. He will pray through us the Word, the will, and the heart of the Father. There have been many times while I was praying for myself or interceding for someone else that I did not know how to pray about or for a situation. All I had to do was ask the Holy Spirit to pray through me. In many instances, when I was struggling the Holy Spirit would reveal a specific Scripture to pray or He gave me insight as to what I should focus my prayer on.

Sometimes, I have been led to worship and praise God for what He had already done instead of asking for anything right away. Whenever I have allowed the Holy Spirit to lead me in prayer it always produced powerful results. My faith and peace increased. I had no fear and no doubts.

Holy Spirit's Wisdom vs Worldly Wisdom

We are bombarded with worldly messages every day through media, what we feed our minds on, and the relationships we build. Often believers don't realize how much they are influenced by these communication avenues instead of the message of the cross. The world's wisdom cannot compare to God's wisdom. But unfortunately many believers are more knowledgeable about the world than the Word of God, therefore they look and respond just like the world.

> The message of the cross is foolish to those who are headed for destruction! But we who are being saved know it is the very power of God. As the Scriptures say, "I will destroy the wisdom of the wise and discard the intelligence of the intelligent." So where does this leave the philosophers, the scholars, and the world's brilliant debaters? God has made the wisdom of this world look foolish. Since God in his wisdom saw to it that the world would never know him through human wisdom, he has used our foolish preaching to save those who believe.
> (I Corinthians 1:18-21)

ASK THE HOLY SPIRIT!

The Corinthian believers, like so many Christians today were trying to live their Christian life on the basis of common sense, which was based on self-preservation. Then and now we want to boast in what we have done instead of giving all of the glory to the Lord.

God said He calls the simple rather than the wise so that no one can boast before Him; God wants us to boast only in the Lord. God, in His wisdom carried out the plan of salvation through the crucifixion and resurrection of Christ, and hid it from those who relied on their own wisdom and education, which he is still doing today. God reveals His plan to those who seek Him.

When I decided I wanted to be led by the Spirit, I went through a spiritual metamorphosis. I was transformed from a religious caterpillar to a Spirit-led butterfly. When the transformation process was complete I no longer viewed people or the world the same. I began to see life through the eyes of God. I am not implying that I am perfect, but I matured and continue to grow in my Christian walk. My life is no longer centered on what I want and what makes me happy. I have surrendered to God and my life is all about what is pleasing to Him and serving His people.

The Holy Spirit showed me how to be healed of my own hurts and low self-worth. He gave me insight about many things that had transpired in my life and were causing me to operate out of a wounded mind and spirit. I was focused on my pain rather than my purpose. I was very defensive because I was fearful of being hurt and rejected. After the Holy Spirit revealed to me how to be healed I asked how I could minister hope and healing to others. God told me to comfort others, as He comforted me.

When the Holy Spirit is in control of our life, wherever we go the atmosphere or spiritual world around us is impacted, because evil always recognizes when one of God's children is present. People will observe our Godly behavior and will want to know who our God is because they see something different in a believer living in the power of the Holy Spirit.

Living in the power of the Holy Spirit means asking the question "Holy Spirit what should I do?" He never stops amazing me with the wisdom He imparts. My life is forever changed because now I access the mind and will of God through His Spirit. I seek the direction of the Holy Spirit in my ministry, marriage, family, friends and everything I do and it has brought me peace that surpasses my understanding. I went from being a frustrated Christian to a Spirit-filled believer whose total dependence is on God. Now I say as Jesus said, "Not my will, but your will be done heavenly Father."

> **I have asked the question "Holy Spirit what should I do?" He never stops amazing me with the wisdom He imparts.**

Chapter 6

Consulting Holy Spirit About Finances

> Yet true godliness with contentment is itself great wealth. After all, we brought nothing with us when we came into the world, and we can't take anything with us when we leave it. So if we have enough food and clothing, let us be content.
>
> (I Timothy 6:6-8)

Money dictates where and how we live, what and how much we buy and, to some extent, our position in the social order. Money also directly impacts our spiritual lives. Our financial state has overwhelming physical, mental and emotional consequences. Money can have tremendous power over how we relate to life and others.

Money is a necessary part of life and it isn't bad or good. The Lord actually owns everything but allows us to be His stewards. When we properly use our possessions and maintain the proper attitude, He will give us more according to His will. When we remember that money is a temporary necessity that loses its importance when we transition to eternity, we will be able to keep it in its proper perspective.

Godliness with contentment provides us with spiritual wealth that material wealth cannot buy. Therefore, when we develop the wrong attitude toward what we are blessed with, it affects us spiritually. When our desires control us, we focus on what we don't have or want. So, we will strive to get more or misuse what has been provided and those who do have more things will spend a lot of time focusing on getting more.

Financial bondage impacts one's attitude, peace of mind, relationships and distracts you from building God's kingdom. When people get bogged down in debt they are hindered in being used by God to bless others. If believers allow the Holy Spirit to lead them in how they use their finances they will never find themselves in debt. This is so important because when weighted down with debt, bill collectors are relentless and it takes the focus off of a believer's relationship with God. It also impacts the ability to stay focused on reading the Bible, praying and fasting. We often become stressed, overwhelmed, and anxious. Paul said, "I have learned how to be content with whatever I have" (Philippians 4:11.)

No matter how much debt you may be in, allow the Holy Spirit to give you direction about how to eliminate it and you will eventually get free. He will reveal what lifestyle changes you need to make and strategies on how to be a good steward of God's blessings. This will always require discipline and sacrificing short-term to become debt free.

Regardless of how someone gets into debt, being in debt can trigger unhealthy emotional responses. One example of how financial problems affect us negatively is in a marriage relationship because it causes tension. Usually in a marriage one person is better with finances than the other.

When couples don't agree on how finances should be handled they become divided, which opens the door for the enemy to come in. As a marriage counselor, I have seen many couples whose relationship has been severely damaged because of unresolved financial issues. It usually stems from one spouse who is not disciplined in the area of spending. Problems can also be a result of only one spouse working and not enough income to cover expenses. There are many more scenarios, but the Holy Spirit can provide a couple with a workable solution to solve these problems if they seek His advice. Too often people are living above their ability to pay the bills. They take on more debt than they can handle because of materialistic wants and desires.

Before I allowed the Holy Spirit to lead me in wisdom, regarding my finances, I found myself struggling over and over again trying to pay bills. The Holy Spirit revealed to me the reason I would often over spend was because I grew up in poverty, which caused me to be materialistic and have an entitlement mentality. I had also made an inner vow when I was a child that when I became an adult I would never be denied the things I wanted, as long as I had money.

Many times I would go into a store to buy a couple of items but I would end up spending more money than I should have because I would pick up items I really didn't need. When I began to listen to the Holy Spirit, He would tell me to put items back that I really did not need and the habit of over spending was broken because I obeyed Him. Now I listen for His leading or ask Him before I pick things up thus eliminating the need to put things back on the shelf.

Therefore, when we obey the Holy Spirit's direction our focus will no longer be materialistic, but instead it will be kingdom focused. The kingdom of God operates on a different system than the world. When we operate according to the guidance provided to us by the Holy Spirit it produces patience, peace, and power in our daily life consistently and an assurance of victory in all things.

Abundance

> But people who long to be rich fall into temptation and are trapped by many foolish and harmful desires that plunge them into ruin and destruction. For the love of money is the root of all kinds of evil. And some people, craving money, have wandered from the true faith and pierced themselves with many sorrows.
>
> (1 Timothy 6: 9-10)

Many Christians have misinterpreted this Scripture and believe it is saying money is the root of all evil. Money is definitely not evil in and of itself, but it is the "love of it."

There are some people who have been blessed financially and debt is not an issue. These individuals need to be led by the Holy Spirit in their finances as well. Whether a person is financially poor, middle-class, or rich, they all need the Holy Spirit to lead them in how to be stewards of what God has provided. God has given us money to do His will, so we ought to be careful with the wealth he gives us. We should use it as the Lord leads us.

Abundance causes some people to be prideful and often these individuals do not depend on God as much because most or all of their physical needs are met. But what they forget is there are some things money cannot buy like peace, joy, love, patience, kindness, etc. These fruit of the Spirit are provided only by the Holy Spirit as we follow his leading. We all know of people who are monetarily rich but are spiritually impoverished.

Wealthy people commit suicide, have problems in their marriages, their children may end up on drugs and many other unfortunate life situations occur that money cannot resolve. Whether rich or poor we all need God's Spirit in order to truly live the abundant life Jesus promised as a result of sacrificing His life on the cross and His resurrection.

> Whether a person is financially poor, middle-class, or rich, they all need the Holy Spirit to lead them in how to be stewards of what they have been given.

Chapter 7

A Spirit Led Marriage

When Christian couples allow the Holy Spirit to lead them in their relationship He will always direct them to follow the Word of God when communicating with their mate. It doesn't matter if the husband or wife had negative or no role models for marriage, the Holy Spirit can teach them how to treat their spouse. The Holy Spirit taught me how to be loving and sensitive to my husband. I no longer focus on making sure my husband is giving me what I need. Instead, I focus on following what the Scripture says my role is in the marriage and depend on the Holy Spirit to guide me. I trust God to talk to my husband regarding what I need as his wife.

Now, my home is more than a place to escape from the world. We all should think of our home as the central headquarters for planning our strategy for kingdom-building. Our homes should be the place where we get together to rest and plan for battle against our enemy – Satan and his followers.

ASK THE HOLY SPIRIT!

Christian homes should be models where the world sees love and harmony. The unsaved should desire to emulate the peace, unity, understanding, and respect they see in godly Christian marriages. That is not to say believers don't have problems in their marriages, but the way they resolve their issues should be totally different from the world.

I have heard many adults and young people say they will never marry because of the poor examples they saw in their parents or other family member's marriages. This is also true because of the examples children have seen in Christian marriages. As a marriage counselor, I have hosted and facilitated couples seminars and unfortunately, what I see over and over again is that many Christian marriages are being torn apart because they are not allowing the Holy Spirit to lead them when problems arise in their relationships.

Problems arise when Christian men do not carry out their God-given responsibilities as the spiritual leader in their home. Some are not even aware of what their roles are because they have never been taught or did not have proper role models when they were growing up.

Some men believe being the head of their home means being the boss over their wife and children, and being served by them, instead of being a servant as Jesus modeled. Thus, they are not following the example of how Jesus treats his bride, the Church. A Spirt filled husband will be willing to lay down his life for his family because he has been given the responsibility by God to be the spiritual leader in his home.

When a Christian wife is unwilling for whatever reason to submit or support her husband in their God given role as spiritual head of the family it hinders peace in the home. I too struggled in this area because I was such an independent person. Because of personal situations and negative relationships with men in my life, I was very rebellious when it came to giving up my control over things. Through prayer and spiritual growth I have been delivered. The Holy Spirit ministered to me about God's order as it relates to delegated authority.

Many women say they want their husband to be the leader in their family, but for various reasons the man refuses to do so. Some men prefer that their wife handle most of the stressful situations that arise in the family. For example, when it comes to paying bills, problems or disciplining the children many husbands and fathers avoid involvement. They feel their primary responsibility is to provide financially for the family.

Usually, when men neglect their leadership role women simply do what they feel they have to do in order to keep things going. This causes women to have a lot of added stress that they should not have to endure. Too many women are carrying excessive mental and emotional weights because they don't allow or encourage their husband to carry their part of the load.

There are some situations that may require immediate attention, but whenever possible, women need to encourage their husband to get involved, even if it is no more than asking their opinion about how they think a matter should be handled.

A husband who is slothful in their duties as head of the household, force their wife to jump in and take control of the home and eventually they become filled with bitterness and resentment in the process. What they often fail to do is ask the Holy Spirit about how to respond in situations like this. If they would tap into their power source, the Holy Spirit and ask him for wisdom, he would give both of them direction from God and they would find peace restored in their marriage and home.

When a Christian husband and wife work out their problems together through the Holy Spirit, it builds a healthy relationship. When they help bear one another's burdens it brings them closer together and the bond between them is strengthened. If the wife maintains a positive attitude and prays for her husband, the Holy Spirit will give her the wisdom about how to approach her husband to discuss family problems and situations. No matter how resistant your husband may be, pray and keep the faith that God will talk to him. It is crucial that Christian couples allow the Holy Spirit to guide them in all marriage and family decisions.

The New Testament contains a wonderful account of a Spirit-filled couple working together for the Lord. Aquila and Priscilla worked diligently together, serving the Apostle

Paul in their home and even traveling from place to place with him. I'm sure every day was not perfect, but they had one main goal to spread the gospel wherever they went. This is a true testimony of a couple who tapped into the power source God has proved to us. The Holy Spirit leading in a marriage is a beautiful thing when a husband and wife join forces to work together to build God's kingdom. Satan doesn't have a chance against a Spirit-filled and Spirit-led couple.

However, there are many Christian spouses who are married to an unsaved or carnal minded mate. Carnal minded people are individuals who profess to be Christians, and may be active in the church, but live worldly lives outside of church activities. A carnal minded Christian may or may not have the knowledge about being led by the Holy Spirit in their household because they have made a choice to ignore or reject the Word. The result of this decision is that they are hardened and not sensitive to the Holy Spirit.

Many spouses who are Spirit-filled and living for God and want to live pleasing lives before the Lord feel the negative pull of their carnal mate. Wives who are faced with this dilemma should conduct themselves according to what the Word of God says.

> Wives, in the same way be submissive to your husband's so that, if any of them do not believe the Word, they may be won over without words, but by the behavior of their wives, when they

> see the purity and reverence of your lives. Your beauty should come from outward adornment, such as braided hair and the wearing of gold jewelry and fine clothes. Instead, it should be that of your gentle and quiet spirit, which is of great worth in God's sight.
>
> (1 Peter 3: 1-4)

The statement "if any of them do not believe the Word" refers to the unsaved husband and it can also be used to describe men who are in the church but are not being led by the Holy Spirit. There are marriages where a husband is saved, but there are many areas where he needs to grow. When women obey this Scripture they will aid in their husband's spiritual growth by their Spirit-filled example. Your life may be the only Bible they are reading right now.

It is important that Christian women be patient and be willing to pray for their husband. I am not saying that a woman who is being physically or verbally abused remain in an unhealthy situation. Nor does this mean she has to divorce her husband. If she chooses to remove herself from a violent or life threatening situation she should continue to pray for him. While separated, the wife should be asking the Holy Spirit what she should do. This principle is the same for men where his wife is a churchgoer but is not Spirit-filled. The husband should seek the guidance of the Holy Spirit as to how to respond to his wife, as he prays for her.

I know of many couples who have been married for years but they don't have peace in their home.

Sometimes the husband or the wife or both stay busy just to avoid one another. Many stay together until their children leave home or tolerate each other until they deem a convenient time to dissolve the relationship. Animosity builds between them because they do not address their issues God's way. Many Christian couples are living together despite being miserable staying together because they believe it is the Christian thing to do. They don't believe that their marriage can change and get better.

I have met pastors, ministers, and deacons who are preaching, teaching, and serving in churches every Sunday, but miserable at home. This is why the door is open for so much infidelity in the church. Satan capitalizes on all the hurt and pain and unhappiness between couples in the church, including leaders, by putting someone in their path that seems to have all the characteristics that are missing in their mate. He orchestrates what seems to be an innocent situation between two hurting or vulnerable people and the rest is history.

When Christian men and women allow the Holy Spirit to guide them as to how to be the kind of spouse God wants them to be, they will see the power of God in their home.

Their relationships will be enhanced and their children will see healthy role models, which will have a positive effect on them when they are ready to start their families. It will also cause the skyrocketing divorce rate among believers to drop. Couples should tap into the power source provided by God, the Holy Spirit, to direct their lives, give them wisdom, and direction regarding what is pleasing to God. When problems and disagreements come up, and every marriage has them, the Holy Spirit will lead them to *WHAT* is right, not *WHO* is right. The Spirit will give them insight into the things that often get in the way of couples understanding one another.

Couples that allow the Holy Spirit to lead in every area of their marriage will have a marriage made in heaven. This is possible because Holy Spirit will teach both of them how to operate in unconditional love when dealing with each other's differences. Marriage typically brings two people together that come from different backgrounds. Each have personal trauma and baggage that they may have not addressed or received healing, but when they ask the Holy Spirit for help they will receive much needed guidance on how to truly become one.

We are living in an era where many believers are justifying living together outside of marriage. Some have told me they don't feel that they need a marriage license to prove anything. Couples living together are of the belief that if the relationship doesn't work out it is easier to walk away if they are not married. But what they don't realize is they develop emotional and spiritual soul ties just like married couples. This is a deception from the enemy to keep believers from following the will of God. We cannot expect to get God's best when we are operating outside of his commandments. Scripture says fornication is wrong and God has not changed his mind regardless of what society condones. God honors the marriage bed not the "test it out bed"!

When problems and disagreements come up, and every marriage has them, the Holy Spirit will give couples wisdom about WHAT is right, not WHO is right.

Chapter 8

Spirit Led Parenting

Parents have life-long and far reaching impact in the lives of their children. Parenting is one of the highest callings a person can have in this life. A parent's influence shapes the world of their children. As godly parents nurture and instruct their children they will be better equipped as they grow up to make life-changing and history-making accomplishments. Therefore, when parents allow the Holy Spirit to lead them in shaping the lives of their children it touches many generations to come.

I am the mother of two beautiful daughters who are now parents themselves. I raised both of my children in a Christian home and with Christian principles. We attended church every Sunday and often during the week, therefore, my children were well acquainted with the Word of God and the ways of God. Even though my daughters knew the ways of God, they, like their parents made life choices that did not always reflect their knowledge of the Word. If I had the knowledge about being led by the Holy Spirit that I have now I would have made much better parenting decisions.

Often Christian parents respond to issues in their children's lives out of their emotions rather than consulting the Holy Spirit. Because of their love for their children they get caught up in the circumstances rather than viewing the problem through the eyes of God. Whenever parents respond that way it literally compounds the problems. They sometimes come to conclusions based on incomplete information or say things to their children that they later regret.

Children learn how to handle conflict by observing how their parents or other adults, they are influenced by, handle their problems and crisis. I can think of times I responded to problems or issues my daughters were faced without asking the Holy Spirit first what I should say or do. I relied on methods I had experienced as a child when my parents responded to things I was going through.

I was blessed with two wonderful parents who I know loved their children, and I had twelve siblings. My parents were not saved for most of our young lives; therefore, they made many mistakes parenting us.

I know if they had been saved and led by the Holy Spirit they would have handled problems that came up differently. I often observed my parents as they were frustrated, overwhelmed and dealing with their own unresolved issues. This impacted me and my siblings in different ways and affected our relationships and marriages. However, for those of us that decided to turn to God for our answers found the better way.

One of the most effective parenting tools is living a Godly life in front of your children. I preached a sermon once to Christian parents titled *"I Can't Hear What You're Saying for Seeing What You Are Doing."* Several of the children in the congregation came and thanked me after the sermon, but interestingly not many parents gave me any feedback. My goal was not to make parents feel guilty, but to help them understand they needed to do more than bring their children to church. Their children needed to see Christ lived out in their parents at home at all times and especially when difficult situations developed.

Christians should be raising their children according to the Word of God, not modeling after the world. Too many Christian parents are raising their children based on the world's standards. They take their children to church, but raise their children according to what the world dictates, without questioning it.

I don't believe any parent wants to give their child advice that is not good for them or respond in a destructive way. Unfortunately, parenting does not come with a manual and many adults didn't have good role models in their parents. It doesn't matter how good or bad of a parenting experience you had growing up; you can have the wisdom needed to be a godly parent because of the power source God promised to his children - Holy Spirit.

The Holy Spirit can direct parents in the area of their child's diet, what they watch on TV, what kind of music they should listen to, the kind of friends they should have, their education, how they should dress, the places they should go, etc. We know that every experience a child encounters is affected by the decisions they make now and in the future that will impact generation after generation. Too often Christian parents base their parenting on how their parents taught them, much of which was not biblically correct. I have heard many believers say, "This is how my mother or father did things, and I am going to do that too." If your parents were not saved or went to church but did not live according to the Bible, be cautious in following their advice. That doesn't mean unsaved people don't know how to parent, it's just important that everything we do as believers lines up with the Word of God.

Then there are people that say, "I am not going to raise my children like my parents raised me." This usually happens with people whose parents were either abusive or excessive in some way; nevertheless, they too were not led by the Holy Spirit. Scripture is clear that we should be raising our children according to the leading of the Holy Spirit. Each child is uniquely designed by God and we need his wisdom to determine what is best for them. I caution parents not to lump all of their children's needs together because what meets one child's need may not suffice for the other one.

There are times when parents have done all the right things but their child still goes astray. I have seen parents whose children decided to use drugs or alcohol even though it was never in their home growing up. Some parents become very upset and feel the child is disrespecting them or making the family look bad. When they respond to situations like this in anger and fail to consider the fact that the real enemy is Satan, it is an indication they have not sought wisdom from the Holy Spirit about how to handle the matter.

Our children are exposed to more things earlier in life than ever before and they have access to things that adults fall victim to when living outside the will of God. When a child begins to go down the wrong path or a parent discovers their child is already participating in behaviors that they did not learn in the home that is the time for Christian parents to seek guidance from the Holy Spirit. The Holy Spirit will give them the wisdom, thereby keeping the parents from losing their peace and joy, despite their circumstances, while interceding before Lord for their child.

I have seen too many Christian parents fall apart when negative things happen in their child's life. Instead of letting go of their faith and belief that God is able to handle any situation, parents need to seek the power source God has given – Holy Spirit. When our faith is tested through our children, they are watching how we respond and it is a great opportunity for them to see our faith in action.

ASK THE HOLY SPIRIT!

I know many parents, like me, wish we would have done things differently when we were raising our children, but all is not lost. Now that we know better we can pass our Spirit-filled wisdom on to our children and grandchildren. Pray and ask the Lord for opportunities to share the wisdom He has given you with other parents.

Adult Children

I often see Christian parents too involved in their adult children and grandchildren's lives. My advice to these parents is to allow their adult children to make decisions that they feel is right for their families; even if they disagree. Or if your child asks for your advice, first consult with the Holy Spirit about what advice to give or if you should offer any suggestion at all.

Even if adult children do not ask for guidance, as parents we can always pray and ask the Holy Spirit to guide our children and grandchildren in their decisions. When we consult the Holy Spirit in how we should interact and respond to our children and grandchildren He will give us divine wisdom. He will strengthen the relationship, instead of making them angry by imposing thoughts and beliefs on them that are not their own.

Whenever we try to impose what we believe on our family members they will resent it and will most likely go in the opposite direction. It is not about who's right but what's right, and we know God is always right. When parents allow the Holy Spirit to lead them it takes away all the stress and pressure of making the right decisions about your children.

Many of the parenting help books are not based on the Bible, therefore, Christian parents should be careful in following their advice. The best advice is always following God's will. Even though parents have two situations that are similar it doesn't mean they should be handled the same way. This is important to remember when there is more than one child because comparing one child to another will cause them great heartache, pain and resentment. Every child is unique and should be treated as an individual. The Bible says comparing ourselves among ourselves is not wise.

When parents make the mistake of favoring one child over another they cause lifelong damage to the child, as it can result in feeling less loved by their parents than their sibling. The Holy Spirit will give parents insight into what each child's needs are and who God created them to be. God said in the Word that he has no favorites. Believers should follow our heavenly Father's advice of loving unconditionally.

When God's advice is not followed, the result can be devastating when teens turn to the world for answers. They can end up in prison, dope houses, chemical addiction programs, mental institutions, prostitution, or death.

ASK THE HOLY SPIRIT!

There are millions of individuals who were damaged as children because parents failed to seek God's wisdom in raising and nurturing them. There are of course exceptions but they are small in number in comparison to people who were simply parented incorrectly. There is hope; the Holy Spirit can teach parents everything they need to know about parenting no matter what the children are going through. I thank God for the guidance the Holy Spirit has given me as a parent and grandparent when I ask Him what to do.

> **Christians should be raising their children according to the Word of God, and by the leading of the Holy Spirit.**

Chapter 9

Spiritual Guidance in Living Single

Christian singles are faced with many challenges and often feel alone when they have to make decisions. Some of the issues Christian singles are faced with are relationships, sexuality, self-esteem, finding God's will, maintaining a passion for God, fear, coping with widowhood, spiritual growth, dating, identity, financial security, living alone, coping with divorce and single parenting.

This list reflects just a few of the overwhelming issues Christian singles face every day. Most of the Christian single women I have encountered are unhappy and focus a lot on how to change their status from single to being married. They often struggle with loneliness, which distracts them in their relationship with God. Many Christian single women are the head of their household raising children without support. They may be the sole source of income for their family, which adds to the weight of all the things they have to cope with as a single person.

Some single Christian women are focused on their relationship with God and are choosing to make him their priority have peace and joy while they wait for God's timing to change their status. This earthly life will have challenges but the choice is to trust and obey God or let the burdens become the focus. Make the choice to utilize the power source God has given each believer – the Holy Spirit to meet all needs, wants, and desires. Problems will come and God is not concerned with what you face but how you face it. Is the Holy Spirit your choice of power to get through difficult times?

Christian single men, as well, have many challenges, but somewhat different from the ones women face. In many cases, men are not usually raising children but there are some who do. Men who are Christian fathers have the challenge of interacting with the mother of their children, and for some this can often be uncomfortable when visiting with their children. Fathers are more likely to have the responsibility of providing child support. Christian single men often date as many women as they like and often feel it is acceptable to fornicate with these women.

Maintaining sanctified relationships, allowing God to lead them in choosing a mate, and taking caring of their own needs are the same challenges for single women. Yes, loneliness impacts both men and women. Men face the pressure of women pursuing them and their desire for pursuing women for sex.

Then singles have the "why are you not married" question from loving friends and family. This can weigh heavily on a single person and can cause them to question and doubt their status. Many begin to ask if there is something wrong with them that they are not married. Even though friends and family have no intention to hurt them it does, and often has negative impacts on their relationship. This is a time for singles to be bold, and not feel it is necessary to explain why they are single, but to praise God for this time in their life to do His will – to own their singleness and shine for Jesus.

If Christian singles allow the Holy Spirit to lead them in their decisions they could impact the world mightily. Being single has many benefits and that fact is often forgotten when Christian singles get so focused on having companionship. Being single, is a prime season in a person's life where they can be really used by God in ministry. Freedom to move as God leads, whether into long term or short term missions, domestic and foreign. This is the time to seek God and allow Him to move in a way that is unique for a single person and how He can use this season in life in a way that a married couple could not be used. The opportunities are endless, seek and you will find the excitement of being single when the Holy Spirit leads.

Dating

As in all seasons of one's life, Christian singles should be consulting the Holy Spirit on the topic of dating. This is one of the easiest areas where singles get out of God's will.

The enemy will bring people into a single's life for the sole purpose of getting them distracted from doing God's work.

Singles should ask the Holy Spirit if they should be dating at all. Just because someone comes along that is interesting does not mean you should get involved with that person. Even giving out your phone number or talking on the phone should be prayed about. Words are powerful and many people have entered into ungodly and unhealthy relationships that started with what seemed like innocent phone conversations. When singles depend on the leading of the Holy Spirit they will be able to discern when the enemy tries to entrap them through temptation, which will lead them out of God's will.

> The temptations in your life are no different from what others experience. And God is faithful. He will not allow the temptation to be more than you can stand. When you are tempted, he will show you a way out so that you can endure.
>
> (1 Corinthians 10:13)

Some singles that have been single for many years get out of God's will because they feel they are getting older and they don't want to be old and alone. They fail to ask the Holy Spirit for his leading. They begin to compromise their Christian values and settle for someone they did not seek God's will on before making a decision. This often results in singles getting into relationships that hinder their spiritual growth and sometimes leads them away from God.

I know a Christian man who had resolved that God wanted him to live a life of singleness. He focused on his education and earned a degree and became a college professor. He was faithful to God and I remember every time I would see him he would have this big smile on his face and he would always greet people by saying "Praise Jesus!" After living a single life for fifty years, he said God had released him to marry and that he had found his soul mate and she too was a believer who had been waiting for God to send her a mate. They got married and he treated her like a queen! I wanted to share this story to encourage women and men who are getting older not to become concerned because if God desires for you to have a mate he will provide one for you no matter how old you are or how long you have to wait.

The Bible says that God has called some people to remain single for the work of the Lord. If God has a call on your life that requires you to remain single He will speak clearly to you regarding His plan for your life. Some individuals struggle with accepting that God has called them to singleness because they don't want to be alone. If God calls a person to live a single life He will give them the grace and peace to do so, if they submit to His will and don't resist the call. God said He will never put more on us than we can bear.

This is not a decision a single person should make based on other people's opinions. This is something that you need to know that God has spoken to you and not someone else giving their advice or opinion. When a person knows that God has spoken to them they will not doubt their decision when relatives and friends began to question them about why they aren't married. They will be able to strongly and confidently say I am single because that is God's call on my life. Whenever we submit our will to God, He will give us joy no matter what situation we encounter.

Choosing a Mate

Ask the Holy Spirit and be led by Him. There are so many stories of believers not consulting God or were disobedient to God's leading when they were choosing a spouse and they suffered tremendously for it. Some people have chosen the wrong mate because they were depending on the advice of a friend, family member, church member, church leader, or willfully disobeyed the leading of the Holy Spirit.

The following scenario is one many will relate to if relying solely on the advice of others.

> A believer seeks the advice of a family member and/or a Pastor when trying to decide if they are making the right choice for a mate. They seek out people they trust or respect for the wisdom needed to be able to discern whether concerns about the person they are

considering to marry are valid or not. Behavior develops in the person they are engaged to that seems abusive. But the people that they entrusted with the information advised them to still marry the person because they liked the person and they had not seen any abusive behavior that should cause any concern. The marriage takes place based on the advice and no one consults the Holy Spirit. The couple stays married for many years and eventually have children. As time passes, the abusive mental and physical behavior escalates and results in divorce. But by the time the marriage ends the physical and emotional damage had been done to the spouse and children. The divorce affects the children negatively and the experience impacts their lives for many years after the breakup. Needless pain and suffering was endured.

If that scenario is real to you, consider the following:

A divorced woman that left an abusive marriage wants to be married again but this time to the right person. Her decision to marry the first time was a decision that did not include God.

She has a new church home and a man in her church approaches her but is known for having relationships with many other women in the church. She decides to seek direction from a church leader about the situation. The leader's advice was that she should pursue a relationship with the man since he wasn't married to anyone yet even though he was dating several women in the church. However, through prayer, she receives confirmation from the Holy Spirit that this leader was not being led by Him. She made the choice to follow the Holy Spirit and needless pain and suffering was avoided.

Seeking the will of God brings wisdom and discernment – Holy Spirit – God's power source will never fail you.

During the dating stage woman are often treated like a queen. Men often start out with opening doors, sending flowers and going out to dinner often. She believes this has to be the man for her. But she finds out that this man had some history of drug use and abuse. She seeks out others for advice and some believers tell her to get out of the relationship and others tell her to do what would make her happy and not to listen to opinions. So, without prayer, she marries the man and it turns into an emotionally abusive relationship and she regrets her decision to marry him. Eventually, the marriage ends in divorce. She is devastated and even has an emotional breakdown. Instead of listening to other believers and following feelings life can turn out differently. With the Holy Spirit, He knows everything and if we ask, listen and obey we will never be out of God's will.

ASK THE HOLY SPIRIT!

LIVING SINGLE

If you are a single person that God has called to live a single life and you are struggling with it, ask the Holy Spirit to help you. God will give you a strategy and peace in dedicating your life completely to his work.

For singles waiting for God to give you the mate he has chosen for you, I encourage you to ask the Holy Spirit to give you the power to live a pure and holy life. You cannot and do not have to do it on your own. If you are a Christian single that is miserable while you are waiting for God or a single that is going from one bad relationship to another, fornicating, and being emotionally damaged over and over again, I encourage you to call on your helper the Holy Spirit. He can show you how to make your single life happy, exciting and holy while you wait on God.

The Christian singles that I have met that truly depend on the Holy Spirit are living holy and fulfilled lives. They are so energetic and focused on what pleases the Lord and trusting God for everything they need. When they begin to feel lonely they run to the arms of God instead of a person. These singles experience the benefits and understand the importance of being led by the Holy Spirit, they don't fear being single they embrace the call God placed on them!

> If Christian singles allow the Holy Spirit to lead them in their decisions such as dating, choosing a mate, and raising their children their lives would be filled with peace instead of turmoil.

Chapter 10

Spirit Led Leaders

Leading a congregation or ministry is one of the most challenging roles for an individual and their family. The responsibility of overseeing and guiding the lives of lost and hurting people is tremendous. There is an estimated 300,000+ protestant churches in the United States with an approximate average of 75 congregants, totaling about 22,500,000 people; all having unique backgrounds, physical, mental and emotional needs expecting their pastors to meet their needs.

Pastors are expected to be involved in not only ministering to these individuals in their local churches, they are also expected to conduct weddings, attend graduations, baby showers, visit hospitals, provide marriage counseling, assist in planning and conducting funerals, conduct business meetings, and more. Pastors also have to prepare and preach weekly sermons and teach Bible study classes. Although some pastors have the luxury of delegating many of these responsibilities and even takes time and attention. Then there is the Pastor's spouse and children who have many needs, as well as other family members vying for their time and attention.

Many leaders experience divorce, poor health, or infidelity, because they perform most of these roles without the leading of the Holy Spirit. They often work long hours, don't get enough sleep and operate out of human logic and emotions when handling day to day issues. Many leaders seek the advice of their family, friends and congregants before asking the Holy Spirit for His wisdom. Though I don't believe this is intentional, it is just that most leaders have not been taught or had no role model who sought the Holy Spirit's leading.

I can sympathize with leaders and the struggles of pastoring a church. My husband and I co-pastored a small congregation in Minnesota for over six years. When I reflect back on that season in our lives, we made many mistakes because we were not being led by the Holy Spirit in every decision we had to make. We loved God and loved his people, but we were often caught off guard by situations that would arise in the ministry. We were often overwhelmed and exhausted by our busy schedules, continuous challenges, and attacks by the enemy. We soon discovered that no matter how much we loved people they came with so many unresolved hurts and needs it seemed we could never do enough.

ASK THE HOLY SPIRIT!

We also discovered a lot about ourselves during this time and realized we too had many unresolved issues and the day to day challenges would cause them to surface. It would seem logical that our prayer life would increase because we knew we couldn't make it without God, but sad to say, we were often too busy and exhausted to pray. What we didn't realize is that we could have avoided situations or handled things in a better way had we asked the Holy Spirit for direction before responding to situations. Instead we waited until things had gotten out of hand or at a crisis point to ask the Holy Spirit to lead us.

My heart goes out to leaders of churches or ministries because I know the price they pay to minister to God's people. I also know much of the pain and pressures leaders deal with is self-inflicted. It is a direct result of them not stopping to take the time to ask Holy Spirit for direction. It is easy for leaders to function outside of the Holy Spirit and allow circumstances to overwhelm them. This happens when leaders unconsciously get so distracted by what they are dealing with that they forget the Holy Spirit was sent to give them direction in resolving matters. There are times too, when their pride or emotions get in the way as well.

I know from experience if leaders would seek wisdom from the Holy Spirit at all times the problems they find themselves embroiled in wouldn't exist or they would have handled them in a totally different manner. Asking the Holy Spirit is something one has to practice. Most believers are not aware that most of the time they operate out of their own human reasoning. They do this because that is what they are familiar with and have practiced it all of their lives so, they do it without even thinking about it. Being led by the Holy Spirit means you have to ask, listen and obey whatever He tells you to do. Often what He tells you to do will be uncomfortable and will not make sense to your intellect. Trusting the Holy Spirit with all decisions is God's plan for your life.

Church leaders should be asking the Holy Spirit to lead them in choosing leaders over groups, selecting musicians, business decisions, fundraising, etc. Pastors have done a lot of damage to their church family because of the people they have placed in leadership. They chose group leaders based on their professional experience or desire to have a position. Sometimes leaders are chosen based on their financial contributions and/or their attendance in church. Small congregations pose the biggest challenge, so the pastor just uses who he has even though he knows they are not qualified or just to keep the few people they have coming back.

Another reason people are given leadership roles is due to their loyalty to the Pastor. I believe it would be safe to say that when asked many pastors would have to admit that they don't pray and ask the Holy Spirit every time for direction when choosing leaders in their churches.

A major mistake a leader can make is to watch what other churches are doing and duplicate it in their ministry. Adding programs that God has not told leaders to incorporate keeps the people in their churches so busy with activities they don't have time to pray and focus on their spiritual growth. It also requires more time away from their families and they end up neglecting the things they need to be doing in their homes.

Women who have husbands that do not have the same belief in God often make the mistake of giving more time to the church than taking care of their first ministry, which is their home and husband. Therefore, the husband feels the church is more important than he is and rejects the church and God.

Pastors and church members get overworked and burn out. Holy Spirit reveals the will of God to our leaders as they pray, seek, and wait on God for direction and wisdom to feed the people seeking a relationship with God in our churches. Is the power source God has provided for the church, regardless of the denomination evident?

Every leader should still be asking the Holy Spirit if their particular denomination is doing what is right for their congregation. When denominational organizational structures were established did the leaders take into account how their rules and guidelines will impact the people? It is up to each Pastor to seek the leading of the Holy Spirit about how to lead the people that have been placed under their care and what is best for the spiritual growth of the members. It is never too late to bring the Holy Spirit into the

Church and diligently seek Him to reveal any shortcomings in your church to bring change that will give the honor and glory to God that He and only He deserves and desires for your Church family.

Stressed out leaders is not God's plan for the Church. When leadership is not following the leading of the Holy Spirit there is only frustration, confusion, and often times defeat. I used to think that leaders were exempt from having a peaceful life because I know many pastors that are worn out, miserable, and complaining about all the problems they were having with the people in their churches. It is not surprising to have leaders who preach eloquent sermons but are not practicing what they want or expect the church family to do. Members see the hypocrisy and copy what the pastor does versus what is preached. Where is the power source God provided for us in our churches?

I have a saying "Satan doesn't care how much Word you know, but how much Word you live." The Scriptures tell us not only to be hearers of the Word, but to be doers, because to be hearers, or "preachers in this case" only, will profit us absolutely nothing if the Holy Spirit is ignored. I saw this in the lives of leaders before I became a pastor, then I saw it happen in my own life.

When I look back over the six years I was a leader I must confess I did not apply all of the wonderful sermons I preached when opposition came in the ministry. I was so busy protecting myself from the attacks that I often forgot

ASK THE HOLY SPIRIT!

the Scripture that says "Our fight is not against flesh and blood, but against principalities, powers and wickedness in high places." (Ephesians 6:12) The reason that happened is I had some unresolved hurt and the enemy knew it, therefore, Satan knew I had an open door that he could walk through over and over again. When I would get hurt by people's responses or actions I did not ask Holy Spirit to guide me. As leaders, we are held to a higher standard and commitment to listen and obey the Holy Spirit, as He tells us the very thoughts of God. God's children could be spared much pain, confusion, and spiritual stagnation, if only we surrender and let the Holy Spirit direct us in what God has planned for us, as His leaders. The distractions of this life would not take our focus off of God. The Church would become alive and reach others with the Good News!

Pastors that are not aware of or don't focus on deliverance they need from things that will distract and disrupt their ministries will fail their members. There are many leaders who struggle with mental health issues but are ashamed to admit it and get the help they need. Everyone has had some kind of traumatic experience in their life that impacted them emotionally and these issues must be addressed because they don't just go away. They become tools for Satan to use to destroy the Pastor and congregation. Some spiritual issues come from generational curses and hereditary strongholds.

Pastors are human and they need to get help just like the people they are trying to help. I believe in the philosophy that hurting people, hurt people, but healed people bring healing to others. Wounded leaders try to bring healing to others without seeking their healing first and without the Holy Spirit it is not possible. What many leaders don't realize is their unresolved issues impact their leadership both directly and indirectly. If Jesus had to spend so much time in prayer to his Heavenly Father, how much more we need to be in prayer, as leaders. His example of being in constant contact with God is what sustained him through the trials and temptations he endured. Jesus understands the pain of leadership and the sacrifice it takes to be the vessel God can use to build His kingdom.

Do you want to have the ministry God has planned for you?

Jesus taught and showed us how to be a leader that will bring honor and glory to the Father. Jesus spent a lot of time praying to the Father, and when He came out from His time of prayer He would always be full of power and was not distracted by the circumstances around Him. Jesus sent the Holy Spirit to empower us to live a holy life so we could be the light of the world and the salt of the earth. As believers and leaders we have a responsibility as God's ambassadors to properly represent Him in the world. I consider it an awesome privilege and honor to be a representative of the Creator of the universe.

God tells us to live according to His Word and trust the Holy Spirit. He knows that without the Holy Spirit our human reasoning will prevent us from being vessels that He can use to build His kingdom here on earth.

ASK THE HOLY SPIRIT!

In order to fulfill God's plan the Holy Spirit will reveal to us the things we need to be delivered from to become effective leaders. Every believer, including leaders, has one or more areas in their life that needs spiritual cleansing. This is not something we can do without the power the Holy Spirit provides for us. Imagine living this earthly life in joy and peace! If that thought seems foreign or just not possible for you rebuke the thought because it is not of God.

When we accepted Christ as our Savior and Lord, we still must live this life in these earthly bodies and our minds have to be continually renewed or transformed to understand God's plan. This transformation can only take place if we consciously allow the Holy Spirit to guide in all things. Leaders should ask the Holy Spirit to lead them daily, as they make decisions about their churches, family matters, and financial matters that impact the lives of many people. If they don't continuously ask the Holy Spirit to lead them, they will make crucial decisions based on their experiences, emotions or the advice of others who are operating outside the will of God.

So, what did Jesus do? He prayed and prayed some more, then He acted when the answers were provided to Him. That same power is active today in the same Holy Spirit.

> And all of this is a gift from God, who brought us back to Himself through Christ. And God has given us the task of reconciling people to Him.
> (2 Corinthians 5:18)

Leaders are ambassadors, role models, messengers and representatives. In our work as Christ's ambassadors we will continuously encounter people and situations that require spiritual wisdom.

The success of every assignment depends on our seeking the wisdom and will of the Father. Too often God tells us to do something and we attempt to carry it out without asking the Holy Spirit to direct us. We have lived life in our own understanding, our own reasoning too long. It is time to start relying on and believing in the power of the Holy Spirit.

Before I began to mature in my Christian life, I would hear God tell me what He wanted me to do but I did not take the time to ask Him for details. One time God spoke to me and said, "Joyce you know when I speak to you about doing something, but you don't stop to ask Me about the when and the how." God gave me the following example to help me understand what He meant.

A mother tells her child, "I want you to go to the store." The child takes off running to the store, but when he gets there he discovers, he didn't ask his mother what she wanted from the store and he didn't get the money to pay for it. So he has to go back home and ask his mother what she wanted and get the money, then go back to the store.

God told me that I was like the little boy in this story. As a result, I often made a lot of mistakes and wasted a lot of

ASK THE HOLY SPIRIT!

time. I had to learn that when I heard God telling me He wanted me to do something, I also needed to stop and shut out the world so I could pray and ask the Holy Spirit to guide me and wait for the specific instructions on how to carry it out.

We cannot be effective messengers and representatives of God if we are not operating according to the leading of the Holy Spirit. Jesus said He was sending the Holy Spirit to us to be our Counselor and our Guide. It is imperative that we rely on the Holy Spirit to teach us, lead us, and empower us if we are going to be effective in teaching and being examples of Spirit-led leaders. Too often we focus on what we can see, touch, and feel. We blame people for the troubles in our churches, homes, relationships and the list can go on and on when the real enemy gets no notice and laughs endlessly at un-empowered believers. We are fighting spiritual battles without the proper knowledge or tools against Satan and his demonic forces. We need the Holy Spirit to equip us so that we will be victorious no matter what situation we encounter. Satan is defeated, but if he can distract the attention off of himself on to those you are called to serve then he has succeeded in keeping the focus on people so they fight and destroy themselves.

> Stop deceiving yourselves. If you think you are wise by this world's standards, you need to become a fool to be truly wise. For the wisdom of this world is foolishness to God....
> (1 Corinthians 3:18-20a)

Worldly minded leaders cannot build God's kingdom because God's kingdom is built on spiritual principles.

Those who are operating outside of the will of God cannot understand God's way of doing things. People of the world follow the standards set by this world's natural wisdom and systems. Many leaders are seeking wisdom through seminary degrees, media, secular books, television talk shows, magazines, horoscopes, etc. Some are even turning to advice offered by different religions and using the knowledge they gain from these sources to guide them in their decisions. This is truly "foolish" considering the fact that leaders have access to the highest wisdom available to man.

The Bible said Solomon was the wisest man that ever lived, and his wisdom came from God. The Lord wants leaders to be guided by the Holy Spirit because He knows that if they are not leaning on the Holy Spirit their worldly, human influences will get in the way of them being available to God to build His kingdom here on earth. God's supernatural wisdom is superior to the wisdom of this world. Settling for the advice of this world sets the stage for failure.

Even though Solomon had the reputation of being the wisest man that ever lived, he decided to stop following God's wisdom and began to look and desire what the world was doing. His heart turned to evil and he suffered the consequences of those decisions. Human desires are powerful and deceive us with a false sense of power and freedom. Near the end of Solomon's life, he lost his devotion to God and became a victim of his own trade agreements.

By custom, in Solomon's era beautiful women were awarded to the most powerful member of a treaty to seal the covenant. Therefore, the influx of wives and concubines in Solomon's court led to his downfall. The large number of foreign women in his court made many demands upon him. He allowed them to practice their pagan religions and idol worship in Jerusalem's holy temple. Solomon's own faith was weakened and he eventually approved of and participated in the idolatrous acts.

Solomon's behavior is seen in many leaders today. They are rationalizing their worldly behavior by saying they are human and make mistakes like anyone else. They reason that we serve a forgiving and merciful God, therefore anything they do will be forgiven by Him.

What they fail to remember is forgiveness does not erase consequences. When we are led by our earthly wants and desires we become entangled with the lifestyles and systems of the world; we will end up just like Solomon; devoted to self and not God.

> Do not love this world nor the things it offers you, for when you love the world, you do not have the love of the Father in you. For the world offers only a craving for physical

pleasure, a craving for everything we see, and pride in our achievements and possessions. These are not from the Father, but are from this world.

(1 John 2: 15-16)

Leaders should be asking God daily to direct their life in all that day has to offer instead of waiting to consult God once there is a crisis. We have to learn how to depend on God before a crisis comes by calling on the Holy Spirit to lead and guide constantly, moment by moment, at all times.

I believe if we ask God and take the time to be sensitive to His leading, all the time, we will not have to be changing our plans and schedules because we will hear what He wants us to do before we make or finalize activities.

As I have confessed before, there have been many times in the past when I didn't ask the Holy Spirit for direction and I made the wrong decisions. Many of these plans caused me to be hurt, miserable, and I even lost my joy. But that is no longer the case, now I consult with the Holy Spirit and things always turn out right!

> If leaders would seek wisdom from the Holy Spirit at all times the problems they find themselves embroiled in wouldn't exist or will be handled in a manner that will bring honor and glory to God.

Chapter 11

Listening for Holy Spirit to Speak

Believers should always be listening for God's voice, as He speaks through the Holy Spirit. This is how God reveals His will to His children. In John 6:38 Jesus said "I came not to do my will, but my Father's will." Every believer should follow the example of Jesus. We should always seek the will of the Father in every area of our lives. In order to hear God we must have an intimate relationship with Him. We must communicate with Him in all things, at all times, by being tuned in to the Holy Spirit.

Effective communication is give and take. Imagine trying to have a relationship with someone who is always talking to you, but never listens to what you have to say. That is what many believers are doing when it comes to God. We pray (talk to God) and tell him everything we want Him to do, but we do not listen or wait to hear what God thinks or wants us to do. We aren't really interested in hearing his opinion because we often have already made up our minds regarding how we want things to turn out.

The Scriptures admonish us to ask God for his wisdom because our goal should always be to do what pleases the Father. The Bible states in 1 Corinthians 7:23, "We have been bought with a price and we no longer belong to ourselves". In other words, when we accept the price Jesus paid for us; the shedding of His blood, dying for our sins, and rising from the dead, Jesus Christ expects us to surrender our life to Him. God has a purpose and plan for every person who accepts His Son as Savior and Lord.

If we fail to listen for God's voice it not only affects us personally but it also affects how we respond and make decisions in both short and long term relationships. Listening for God's voice through the Holy Spirit keeps the body of Christ – Believers, whole and functioning as Jesus had planned for us, both individually and collectively. Just as our physical body has many parts, so it is with the body of Christ – the Church. When one part of our physical body is hurting the rest of the body knows and feels the effect. It is the same for the Church.

The Church is ineffective when not operating under the power of the Holy Spirit. When we listen for God's voice we are able to respond to the needs of others in a way that pleases the Lord and relationships are restored. However, when we choose to go outside of God's will, we and others will suffer the consequences. An example of this is when

God wants to use someone to give a message to another believer. If the person God wants to minister through is not listening for him to speak or is distracted by the cares of this world, they could miss their assignment to minister to a person in need. However, if believers act on the will of God there is a blessing to both the giver and the receiver. Holy Spirit only tells us what the Father's will is and that guidance is perfect.

We can know what God is thinking because He reveals it to us through the Holy Spirit. God wants to share deep secrets about who He is and what He wants to do in the world through His children. God has a flawless master plan for us. However, believers often rack their brains trying to come up with ideas, programs, events, etc., in the name of doing work for God. It was such a relief when I found out that I didn't have to struggle to come up with ideas or plans to do my part in building God's kingdom. God's plan is flawless!

One day, the Holy Spirit told me it was not necessary for me to struggle to live a Christian life, because Jesus had already done the hard part. All God wanted me to do was get my instructions from Him and obey His instructions. When I understood this, my Christian life was no longer hard or difficult. When I pray for God's direction and obey His leading, my life is filled with peace because He tells me exactly what, when, and how to do His will. When we obey, we know that the Father is pleased.

ASK THE HOLY SPIRIT!

The key to obedience is to listen and wait for instructions. For example, in order to know what our natural parents, spouse, or friends want us to do we must listen for their instructions or have a conversation with them. The same is true with our heavenly Father; if we want to know what His will is we must listen for His instructions. This requires us to ask Him through prayer what He wants us to do and be willing to wait for Him to respond.

Often believers say they are doing a work for God, they have never asked God if what they are doing is what He wants. Getting in touch with God would be advisable.

God says obedience is better than sacrifice. No matter how many times we sacrifice our time and talents doing "good" things, if it's not what He wants, God is not pleased with our sacrifices. Jesus said if your Father is truly God, you will gladly listen to His words.

Some believers claim God as their heavenly Father but lack a personal relationship with Him. It is of utmost importance to look to the heavenly Father for wisdom and guidance that comes as a result of studying God's Word and prayer. If He is truly your heavenly Father you will begin to think like God, talk like God, and act like God, as your relationship develops. It will be evident in your lifestyle and behavior that you are being conformed to His image. Living as the world lives will become uncomfortable and your desires will change.

Believers can stumble with being conformed because they have yet to understand how the Holy Spirit will work in their life. God's thinking is so opposite of what the average human thinks. When the Holy Spirit leads the result is hearing God's thoughts and living an abundant life, free of the worries of this world. That is why it is so important that we get God's direction about everything.

Sometimes believers are unaware of how much they have been influenced by the opinions of man. Therefore, daily we should be asking the Holy Spirit to direct us in all decisions to ensure we stay on the path God has ordered. When believers pray and get God's response and obey His direction they can avoid making decisions that have negative consequences. If we trust God with our life and believe that He always knows what is best for us, we will avoid a lot of the pain and heartache that we bring upon ourselves.

The Scriptures tells us that our human reasoning and God's Spirit are always in conflict. In order to trust the Lord with all our hearts, we cannot trust in our own wisdom or the wisdom this world bombards us with constantly.

Results of Listening for God's Voice

- *We stay in the will of God*
- *We avoid making unnecessary mistakes*
- *Abundant peace and joy*
- *Cease from causing pain and suffering to others*
- *Intensify our spiritual growth*

ASK THE HOLY SPIRIT!

> My dear brothers and sisters, be quick to listen, slow to speak...
>
> (James 1:19a)

I used to think this Scripture verse meant to be quick to listen to man and slow to speak. God gave me His interpretation, which is, we should be slow to speak, so we can hear what the Spirit is saying so He can instruct us on how or if we should respond. If we do this we will answer people according to what the Holy Spirit tells us to say instead of giving our own opinions. This will also help us avoid getting caught up in someone else's issues. Sometimes the Holy Spirit will tell you not to respond at all. The key is to listen, wait, and then act.

> Indeed, we all make many mistakes. For if we could control our tongues we would be perfect and could also control ourselves in every other way.
>
> (James 3:2)

God always wants to speak to us regarding all things in our life because He loves us unconditionally and wants the best for us. However, if we get too busy living our lives without seeking or listening to what God's is saying, we miss out on blessings and risk grieving the Holy Spirit. If you encounter life moment by moment, one day at a time and choose to tap into the power source Jesus provided in the Holy Spirit, you will be amazed what God does in and through you!

> We can know what God is thinking because
> He reveals it to us through the Holy Spirit.

Chapter 12

Patience to Wait

The one fruit of the Spirit that we must allow to work in our lives if we are going to follow the leading of the Holy Spirit is the fruit of PATIENCE. We often hear the Holy Spirit speak something to us and then we rush off and attempt to carry out what He has revealed without having the patience to wait to get specific instructions.

When I was an immature believer God would tell me something He was going to do and I would get excited and start telling everyone and begin planning how I was going to make it happen according to what I believed God was saying to me. In my Christian walk God speaks to me through the Spirit about things He either wants me to do or things He has planned for me. However, I needed to grow in my understanding that what God's will looked like to me was not always what it looked like to Him. I also had to understand that God's timing was not my timing.

Many believers become impatient after they have prayed about something and sometimes begin to complain or start doubting. When we pray we must have faith and trust God no matter how long it takes.

Sometimes God answers immediately and other times He chooses to delay in fulfilling our requests. It is important that we remember delay doesn't mean denial. God's timing is always perfect!

Having the fruit of patience is critical if we are going to be led by the Holy Spirit, because it is the only way for us to move according to His leading. If we fail to wait until the Spirit has given the appropriate instructions and we act to quickly we will be out of God's will and the Holy Spirit will not be able to support us with His power and wisdom. Holy Spirit will never move before God says move because they work in perfect harmony. The Holy Spirit's anointing will not rest on us in any situation where we move outside of God's timing. Repentance is the only way to restore the relationship with God and His Holy Spirit.

When God speaks to us about what He wants to do in our lives we must have patience so God can develop the character needed to fulfill the plan He has for our life. God will often reveal things to us that He knows will not manifest immediately because He knows what needs to take place before His plan actually happens. One example of this is when Moses knew God was going to use Him to deliver His people, but Moses got ahead of God and killed an Egyptian.

Moses had to flee and was on the back side of the desert for forty years. Moses was chosen by God to lead the children of Israel out of Egypt at birth, but God used the desert season to prepare him for the task.

When God speaks to a person about a particular call he has on their life to become an evangelist, pastor, or missionary domestic or foreign it doesn't necessarily mean he wants them to do it immediately. The Scriptures tells us unto whom much is given, much will be required. (Luke 12:48) God will never send you to do a task for him unprepared. He knows what is in all of us and what it will take to prepare us to fulfill his plan.

We also have the perfect example in the life of Jesus. At the age of 12, in the book of Luke, Chapter 2, verses 41-52 is the account of Jesus, as a boy preparing for His future. He was in the temple sitting among the religious teachers, listening to them and asking questions all in preparation for His future ministry. His parents had left the temple to join the caravan returning to Nazareth but didn't know Jesus had stayed behind in Jerusalem. When they didn't find Him in the caravan they returned to the temple in Jerusalem.

> His parents didn't know what to think. "Son" his mother said to him "why have you done this to us? Your father and I have been frantic,

> searching for you everywhere. "But why did you need to search?" He asked. "Didn't you know that I must be in My Father's house?" But they didn't understand what He meant. Then he returned to Nazareth with them and was obedient to them. And his mother stored all these things in her heart. Jesus grew in wisdom and in favor with God and all the people.
>
> (Luke 2:48-52)

At a young age Jesus knew what His purpose was, but He did not begin His ministry until He reached the age of thirty. Jesus allowed the fruit of patience to have its perfect way in Him as He waited for God's timing to begin His ministry.

Along with listening for the voice of the Holy Spirit it is critical that we learn how to be patient, once we have heard him speak. We must wait for God's method, timing and provision for the vision He has for each of us.

We have come into a prophetic era again that will require more than ever that we listen and wait with patience on the leading of the Holy Spirit. We must move strategically according to God's master plan for this season. There are going to be so many things happening very quickly and believers must be sensitive to the leading of the Spirit to be effective in whatever capacity God wants to use us in building God's Kingdom in this season.

> The one fruit of the Spirit that we must allow to work in our lives if we are going to follow the leading of the Holy Spirit is the fruit of PATIENCE.

Chapter 13

Hindering the Power Source

In these two passages of Scripture fire is symbolic of the Holy Spirit.

> ...he shall baptize you with the Holy Ghost, and with fire.
> (Matthew 3:11)

> Then, what looked like flames or tongues of fire appeared and settled on each of them. And everyone present was filled with the Holy Spirit and began speaking in other languages, as the Holy Spirit gave them this ability.
> (Acts 2:3,4)

Fire is an indicator of the presence of God. It is symbolic of both judgment and purification. Tongues of fire appeared above the disciples' heads in the upper room on the day of

Pentecost. Fire, when applied to metal, separates the impure from the pure. Fire purifies and cleanses.

When a believer sins against God and follows his or her own earthly desires it grieves the Holy Spirit. To grieve the Holy Spirit means to act in a manner that goes against what God has written in his Word, whether it is in thought or in both thought and deed. Whenever we grieve the Holy Spirit we quench the fire of God in our lives. The Holy Spirit's power never diminishes, but when we bring sorrow to Him it limits His ability to flow through us.

> And do not bring sorrow to God's Holy Spirit by the way you live. Remember, he is the one who has identified you as his own, guaranteeing that you will be saved on the day of redemption.
> (Ephesians 4:30)

When we accepted Jesus Christ as Savior and said to Him we wanted to be His disciples, we were saying we are willing to leave our old life behind and become like Him. This lifestyle change doesn't happen overnight but we are expected to change the way we lived before we knew Him.

I have observed so many individuals who proclaim to be believers but don't change their lifestyles. There have been people who told me they were Christians and I was shocked because of the things I observed them doing. Jesus said come as you are, be He didn't intend for us to stay that way. There are believers who feel it is okay to continue to indulge in drugs, alcohol, immoral sexual relationships, lying, adultery, etc. The Lord knows we are going to be tempted by the enemy and that is why He sent His Holy Spirit to give us power over temptation, but we have to ask the Holy Spirit to help us. We are God's children and His representatives. When people see us they should see Christ in our character and behavior. Therefore, temptation is an opportunity to allow the power source God provided for us – Holy Spirit – to lead you away from sin. Evil is defeated when the Holy Spirit is in control of your life.

However, when we consciously choose to ignore the power the Holy Spirit provides over temptations we sin. We willingly decide to live this earthly life outside the will of God and hinder God's power source –Holy Spirit – from working in and through us.

Lying and Deception Hinders the Spirit

Being engaged in God's truth and choosing to deny human reasoning requires the Holy Spirit to have control in your life. All deception and untruths need to be put away.

> So stop telling lies. Let us tell our neighbors
> the truth, for we are all parts of the same body.
> (Ephesians 4:25)

Jesus said the Holy Spirit is the Spirit of "Truth."

A believer who lies is grieving the Spirit and hinders their ability to hear Him speaking truth to them through God's Word and prayer.

Anger Hinders the Spirit

> And don't sin by letting anger gain control over you," Don't let the sun go down while you are still angry, for anger gives a mighty foothold to the Devil.
> (Ephesians 4:26-27)

There are many believers who struggle with the spirit of anger because of the hurt or disappointments they have experienced. There are Christians who are still angry with their husband or wife because their trust was violated for various reasons. You have children angry with parents and parents angry with their children. Many believers are angry with their leader or people in their congregation.

Anger is an emotion God gave us but He said we must not let it gain control over us because it opens the door for evil to wreak havoc in our minds, hearts, and spirits. In order to stay angry with someone you must continue to think negative and toxic thoughts. Eventually anger turns into bitterness, resentment and sometimes hate. That is why God said we must get rid of it before the sun goes down. Sometimes people feel if they stop being angry with someone who has hurt them they will be letting them off the hook and not holding them responsible for what they had done.

According to Dr. Caroline Leaf, author of *Who Switched Off My Brain? Controlling Toxic Thoughts and Emotions*, anger affects the human body in the following ways:

- Headaches
- Digestive imbalances
- Insomnia
- Anxiety
- Depression
- High blood pressure
- Skin problems, including eczema
- Heart attack
- Stroke

When we chose to remain angry the enemy is happy because he knows the destruction that is taking place in the body. Satan also knows that when a person is angry they will struggle with having the desire to ask the Holy Spirit for help to overcome the anger. Anger blocks our ability to hear the Holy Spirit's leading. That is why God warned us to get rid of all bitterness, rage, anger, harsh words and slander.

<u>Using Profanity Hinders the Spirit</u>

What we speak and how we speak it is either an encouragement or a curse.

ASK THE HOLY SPIRIT!

> Don't use foul or abusive language. Let everything you say be good and helpful, so that your words will be an encouragement to those who hear them.
>
> (Ephesians 4:29)

It is also, amazing how many believers still use profanity. The dictionary defines the word "curse" as a means to call evil down on something or someone. Believers are not aware when they use profanity the enemy is using their words to do his work in proclaiming evil over the person they are "cursing." The Holy Spirit is hindered in the life of a believer who uses foul or abusive language to express their anger or displeasure with someone.

> Get rid of all bitterness, rage, anger, harsh words, and slander, as well as all types of malicious behavior. Instead, be kind to each other, tenderhearted, forgiving one another, just as God through Christ has forgiven you.
>
> (Ephesians 4:31-32)

> Let there be no sexual immorality, impurity, or greed among you. Such sins have no place among God's people.
>
> (Ephesians 5:3)

Thoughts are just as damaging as actions. Quenching and grieving the Holy Spirit hinders believers from having a Spirit filled lifestyle. The Holy Spirit creates in our heart God's purity.

The Holy Spirit creates in our heart the passion and fire of God. He gives us the passion that motivates us to speak the Word of God boldly. God's presence and power will flow through us to touch the lives of people and deliver them from the power of the enemy. The Holy Spirit wants to express Himself in our actions and attitudes. If believers allow the Holy Spirit to direct our actions, we will never suppress or quench the Spirit. We must let the Holy Spirit do the work He was sent to do in our lives.

> The Holy Spirit's power never diminishes;
> but when we bring sorrow to Him it
> limits His ability to flow through us.

Chapter 14

Desires

If we know that the Holy Spirit will give us the right answer every time, why don't we ask him every time? Have you ever asked the Holy Spirit to help you with something and He answered immediately? I have often asked the Holy Spirit to help me when I can't find something, confused about something, or in need of direction about how to do something. In each instance, I asked and the Holy Spirit and He answered me instantly. However, depending on the circumstance, it may take more time in prayer for an answer, but God always answers. Regardless of when the answer is received, Jesus sent us someone who could give us God's wisdom. We can mistake proof our lives if we ask the Holy Spirit to lead us.

One day, I was asking the Holy Spirit to help me find some earrings and of course He showed me where they were. Then He asked me a question. Joyce you have asked me so many times to help you with things and I have always helped you, so why don't you ask me about everything? I heard Him and it brought me to a greater awareness of Him in my life.

I have been reading and studying about the Holy Spirit for over twenty-five years. As a result, I wrote a manual titled *How to Walk in the Spirit/Holy Spirit What Should I Do?* In addition, I have been teaching a Bible study for many years that is focused primarily on discipleship, deliverance and the importance of being led by the Holy Spirit. I asked the Holy Spirit why some believers know so much about being led by the Holy Spirit and how powerful He is but don't ask Him to lead in all things. He told me the problem is when our desires are not God's desires we don't want to ask for His wisdom and guidance. We don't want to hear the answer He may give us. In some instances the Holy Spirit has already given us God's answer but we ignore it and try to convince ourselves that our way is the right or better way.

> *Don't be impressed with your own wisdom.*
> *Instead, fear the Lord and turn away from evil.*
> *(Proverbs 3:7)*

We won't follow the leading of the Holy Spirit if our desires are not God's desires. In order to get back into the will of God and to know God's desires we must first seek His forgiveness and make a decision to actually change. Then regularly pray, read and study the Bible to gain understanding given by the Holy Spirit.

When we read the Bible without the Holy Spirit we are not focused on God's desires, but instead we will find Scriptures to justify our own desires. We must confess and repent as the Holy Spirit brings to mind the things that God has not been pleased with; sometimes they are things that are in us because of hereditary strongholds, bondages, and curses over one's life.

Determining what God desires in specific situations may require pray and fasting as well, because too often we are distracted by our own desires and the desires of others. But when we get alone with God and seek His divine will, we cannot be deceived by the enemy and we can avoid the negative consequences that happen when we get out of God's will.

> Trust in the Lord and do good. Then you will live safely in the land and prosper. Take delight in the Lord, and he will give you your heart's desire. Commit everything you do to the Lord. Trust him, and he will help you.
>
> (Psalm 37:3-5)

The Lord wants to give us the desires of our hearts as long as they line up with His desires. At times in my life there have been things I desired but God did not grant them to me because He wanted what was best for me. When I learned to trust in the Lord and believe that when God says "no" it is because He is concerned about His will being done in my life and will not give me something that will ultimately keep me from fulfilling His purpose and plan for my life. I used to be the kind of person who wanted what I wanted no matter the consequence. I was rebellious and I thought I knew what was best for me and all I wanted God to do was grant my wishes. I can tell you I suffered many painful consequences during that time of my life. But now, I trust God with all of my heart, with all things. Whenever God says "no" I readily say, "Ok Daddy God, because I know You want what is best for me."

As Christians, we are in a spiritual battle daily even though we cannot physically see the attacker. We have a relentless, cunning, and evil enemy whose sole purpose is to get us out of God's will. That enemy is Satan. He is well aware that a believer who is being led by the Spirit is a threat to the works of his demonic kingdom. The only way we will destroy the works of the Devil in our lives and lives of others is to live in the power of the Holy Spirit, at all times.

Victory is achieved by allowing the Holy Spirit to give us God's strategies for each situation. The Holy Spirit will give us specific directions that always result in victory when we obey Him.

> Those who are dominated by the sinful nature think about sinful things, but those who are controlled by the Holy Spirit think about things that please the Spirit.
>
> (Romans 8:5)

When we are controlled by the Spirit, He will dominate our thoughts, attitudes and actions. We cannot be dominated by the Spirit and human reasoning or our wants and desires at the same time. Whatever controls us will be the dominating influence and it will exercise its power over us.

In order for the Holy Spirit to lead us, He must have the greatest influence in our lives and we must give Him complete control. He will lead us around the pitfalls of the enemy when we obey and will always lead us according to God's will.

> How do you know what your life will be like tomorrow? Your life is like the morning fog, it's here a little while, then it's gone. What you ought to say is, "If the Lord wants us to, we will live and do this or that." Otherwise you are boasting about your own plans, and all such boasting is evil.
>
> (James 4:14-16)

There will be times when Holy Spirit will lead in a particular direction and our knowledge and experiences will make us feel it should be just the opposite. We must trust the Holy Spirit, even when it doesn't feel comfortable. We live in a world that encourages us to do whatever feels good. Satan's goal is to get us to sin by tempting us to do what pleases ourselves even if it means consciously disobeying God.

ASK THE HOLY SPIRIT!

> Remember, it is sin to know what you ought to do and then not do it.
> (James 4:17)

Holy Spirit empowers us to overcome any temptation but we must be willing to allow Him to be in control of our emotions and behaviors. We must trust and allow the Holy Spirit to guide us in order to defeat what the earthly life craves. God will never lead us to please our natural desires because it is the opposite of His will. The Holy Spirit is always at war with earthly desires and demonic forces. Anytime our human reasoning is leading it is for certain we will be out of God's will.

> So I say, let the Holy Spirit guide your lives. Then you won't be doing what your sinful nature craves.
> (Galatians 5:16)

We must change our worldly desires to God's desires in order to listen, hear and obey the Holy Spirit. Jesus said He was sending the Holy Spirit and the Holy Spirit would only say what Jesus tells Him to. When Jesus was here in the flesh His desires were always what His Heavenly Father desired. Jesus is our example of what it means to walk in the Spirit at all times and to deny the power of the flesh.

> When the Spirit of truth comes, he will guide you into all truth. He will not speak on his own but will tell you what he has heard. He

will tell you about the future. He will bring me glory by telling you whatever he receives from me. All that belongs to the Father is mine; this is why I said, "The Spirit will tell you whatever he receives from me."

(John 16:13-15)

Jesus knew believers would not be able to function in power and victory without the power of the Holy Spirit. He told the disciples before He ascended back to heaven that He was going away, and He would send them and future believers the Counselor and Comforter to give them power and to lead them into all truth. The power source – Holy Spirit knows God's master plan for each believer's life.

Now that I truly understand all that the Holy Spirit makes available to me, being led by the Spirit in all I say and do is the only option for my life. I don't want to miss anything that I have been given access to by my heavenly Father and His son Jesus. I am committed to spend the rest of my life yielding to the Holy Spirit so that I will experience blessings and victory in every area of my life. I challenge you to join me. Together, as believers, we can impact this world and turn it around with the good news about Jesus Christ, the Kingdom of God, and the power source to do this is through the Holy Spirit.

> We won't follow the leading of the Holy Spirit if our desires are not God's desires.

Chapter 15

The Power Flowing Through Me

Believers, the message of Jesus Christ is to let the world know that through the knowledge and wisdom of the Holy Spirit we can experience complete victory, as we wait for Jesus to return. Unfortunately, too many believers are failing to use this great superpower that Jesus sent to us. This power is greater than any natural weapon. There are examples in the Scriptures of God using individuals who were given this power to overcome governments, armies, nations and religious systems. We can reflect on David and Goliath, Moses and Pharaoh, Elijah and the Prophets on Mount Carmel, Sampson and the Philistines, Jesus, Paul and the Apostles just to name a few.

God's power is the ultimate power! What believers are either not aware of or they lose focus on is that everything starts in the spirit realm and manifests in the natural. There are only two spirits that are operating in the spiritual realm; good and evil, God and the Devil. Individuals are either being led by one or the other; there is no middle ground. The only power that is greater than Satan's power is the Holy Spirit.

Even though my parents didn't go or take me to church I would ask people to take me with them. I did not grow up in a Christian home therefore everything was new to me after I accepted Jesus Christ as my Savior. When I was introduced to Jesus at age 16, I was told if I gave my life to Jesus He would save my soul and make everything all right. Church became my refuge.

Church always fascinated me when I did go because I would hear all of these great sermons and testimonies. At the age of 17, my high school homeroom teacher was a believer and she would take me to her church services. They were lively and people seemed to be pretty happy. So, I thought to myself I want what they have.

After I accepted Christ into my life, even though I had the Holy Spirit living in me, I still lived a defeated Christian life. Since I didn't grow up in the church, I just started watching what the people around me were doing and I mimicked their behavior. I didn't understand that I should depend on this great power source to lead and guide me because it was not explained in a way I could understand it. I would hear Christians talking about how great the Holy Spirit was and what He was doing in their lives, but they did not explain "how" it took place.

Church was very important to me and I would go every time the doors were open for any service. If there was a revival that lasted five days I would be there every night because I knew I would feel good while I was there. I heard a lot of fiery and inspirational sermons, but when I wasn't in church and problems would arise I didn't respond according to how the sermons said I should. I still had a lot of negative issues that plagued me. When I responded in the wrong way or made mistakes I would feel guilty but I didn't know how to change.

I spent a lot of time repenting at the altar for the same things over and over again. I gave Christ my life hundreds of times. Even though I felt guilty, my attitude and decision making wasn't improving very much. I also had a lot of hurt and disillusionment in the church I attended because I thought church people were supposed to be perfect or at least close to perfect, even though I wasn't.

The more I went to church I began to hear and see more negative things. At one point, I wanted to walk away from the church because it no longer was providing me as many "good feelings". Satan made sure I knew about the shortcomings of people in the church, from the pulpit to the back door. Then my Christian life started to feel painful instead of powerful.

I read and heard the following Scripture quoted over and over again in the church:

ASK THE HOLY SPIRIT!

> For we are not fighting against flesh-and-blood enemies, but against evil rulers and authorities of the unseen world, against mighty powers in this dark world, and against evil spirits in the heavenly places.
>
> (Ephesians 6:12)

What I did not understand was that the only way these spiritual enemies could be defeated was through the power of the Holy Spirit. I also did not know how that was to take place in believer's lives. I had no knowledge or understanding about this unseen and dark world. I heard a lot of messages on what I should do as a believer, but not about *how* to carry it out in my daily life.

Another topic I heard many sermons and teachings about was on the fruit of the Spirit and how important it was that the fruit be manifested in my life. I was told or it was implied that I had to produce the fruit. My understanding was that I had to constantly do a fruit inspection in my life to see if I had all nine operating in me. I remember becoming weary because it seemed every time I would do my fruit inspection I was coming up short by a few and sometimes I would only have a couple out of the nine that I could see.

I didn't understand until 39 years later, the Holy Spirit taught me that I was never expected to produce the fruit, but instead the Holy Spirit was to produce it in and through me when I gave him control. This was the greatest revelation of my life because I was trying so hard to produce spiritual fruit in my own strength. I became so excited, I started telling every believer I could because I wanted them to experience this freedom, too. I wanted them to know we don't have to struggle to live the Christian life because we have the power source – Holy Spirit living within us that does what we could never do on our own.

Once I received the understanding about the power source – Holy Spirit, it opened a whole new world to me regarding the spiritual realm. I began to operate on a whole new level. I transitioned from seeing the world through human reasoning to operating in the Spirit. I no longer blamed people or depended on people in day to day life situations.

Now, I understand how the Holy Spirit works. I am unstoppable and unmovable in my stand for God and in the work God has called me to do for His kingdom. I have peace instead of frustration; I have access to the intelligence of God every day, all day. I don't have to wait to get to church to find out how God is thinking; I just tap into my power source – Holy Spirit who knows everything about everything and he gives me God's answer every time. Believers when we depend on the Holy Spirit's power to direct us, we will impact the world in ways we never imagined.

> **Individuals who are led by the Holy Spirit are used by God to bring about transformation wherever they go.**

PAUL'S MESSAGE OF WISDOM

When I first came to you, dear brothers and sisters, I didn't use lofty words and impressive wisdom to tell you God's secret plan. For I decided that while I was with you I would forget everything except Jesus Christ, the one who was crucified. I came to you in weakness— timid and trembling. And my message and my preaching were very plain. Rather than using clever and persuasive speeches, I relied only on the power of the Holy Spirit. I did this so you would trust not in human wisdom but in the power of God.

(I Corinthians 2:1-5)

But it was to us that God revealed these things by his Spirit. For his Spirit searches out everything and shows us God's deep secrets. No one can know a person's thoughts except that person's own spirit, and no one can know God's thoughts except God's own Spirit. And we have received God's Spirit (not the world's spirit), so we can know the wonderful things God has freely given us. When we tell you these things, we do not use words that come from human wisdom. Instead, we speak words given to us by the Spirit, using the Spirit's words to explain spiritual truths.

(I Corinthians 2:10-13)

Ask the Holy Spirit!
The POWER Source JESUS Provided

Printed in the United States
By Bookmasters